"That which is hateful to you, do not do to your fellow. That is the whole Torah; the rest is the explanation; go and learn it."

Rabbi Hillel
Talmud, Shabbat 31a

*For my mother
who taught me to look
for beauty everywhere;*

*And for my father
who showed me the pleasure
of being alive.*

*I dedicate these memoirs to
my parents, my brother,
my grandparents, aunts, uncles
and many cousins, all of whom
perished in the Holocaust.*

"I was lucky to have been surrounded by my family for the first 15 years of my life. Their love and devotion was a great influence on the development and shaping of my character. They imbued me with moral and ethical values and a love of life. It was this foundation that helped me pick up the pieces of my shattered life after the war; to marry and build a new family and to bring children into the world to make it a better place for humankind. History is like a force behind us dictating the way we live our lives. I have to record my part of history, which is the force that kept me going."

Ruth Wachner Pagirsky
June 2013

My father's last words to me were the last time I heard his voice. He had intoned the priestly blessings and then said the following:

"Du mein Kind, Du wirst leben um das Alles zu erzehlen."

"You my child, You shall live, you shall live to tell it all."

AND THIS IS MY STORY.

I started writing my memoirs a very long time ago. I began almost immediately after the war. Most of these early writings are contained in a notebook. I wrote down memories as they came to mind, just to keep the memories alive, never with a thought of actually publishing. My writing increased as I got older, had children and wanted to pass on to them the legacy of my life and my experiences during the war. I carry the pictures of life and death in the vault of my memory unchanged and undiluted by time. Often I would be awakened by nightmares and propelled out of bed, running. Running to nowhere, just following the bad dreams and then finding myself in the kitchen and waiting for my heart to stop racing. Then I would sit down and write. It helped. Later on, starting in 1977, I spent five summers at Kibbutz Parod as a volunteer. I would sit in the quiet afternoons, let my mind wander and let the memories surface. Sometimes they were memories and sometimes I wrote in the form of a diary as I allowed my thoughts and feelings to drift.

Being the only member of my family who witnessed the atrocities, and having survived the Holocaust, I feel a sense of obligation to record the events which led to the demise of my family.

I keep them alive. I am a remnant of a time past, a lost world. I think of myself as a custodian of the cultural identity of my people; their tradition, language, their very way of life. Now, in the autumn of my life, I would like to pull all my writing together and have it published. Not necessarily for the general public, but mostly for my children, grandchildren and all those yet to come. We construct memory in the present and by doing so we create our identity. Remembering where I came from defines who I am now. I know that it will take a long time to do this and I hope that I will be granted the emotional and physical strength to complete it.

"Only I alone escaped to tell thee." (Job)

Regina and Jehoshua Wachner (1922)

My brother Benjamin was born March 15, 1925. He was a beautiful child, chubby with a head full of blond hair and big blue-gray eyes that were (I was told) serious even as a baby. Almost as if he knew from birth what the future had in store for him.

I was born a year later on May 8, 1926, scrawny almost to the point of transparency, a poor sleeper and poor eater. In spite of this, I was a child born with a smile and laughter. I was often told that to my father the sun rose and set with my smile. I have no memory of growing up without Benno (short for Benjamin). We lived in Berlin, Germany, in a very nice, rather elegant section that was called Charlottenburg, on Kantstrasse 38. We had a large apartment that was bright and sunny, and Benno and I shared a room. Benno used to invent games; tie me up with chord and then come to my rescue when I had enough, or he would make sails out of blankets and we would pretend that we are at sea in a boat, which was my crib. I must have been about three or four years old but I do have a clear picture of some of these games. Cousins and friends used to visit but my place was always next to Benno. He would often tease me but he was always there to watch over me and make sure that no hurt came to me. We were separated only once. I was a sickly child and suffered from severe asthma. When I was eight years old I was sent to a Jewish (kosher) sanatorium at the North Sea in Vyck auf Foehr on the island of Amrum. I was there for six months and came home cured. I was homesick, no visits were permitted, but I also have very fond memories of the other children, some much sicker then I, and the very kind and loving staff. I came there in March 1934 and it was quite cold. Yet every morning after our lessons (we had school for three hours) we would bundle up and walk to the beach. As the weather got warmer we walked barefoot in the sand exercising our toes, and collected shells, which we painted and decorated when we got back to the home.

Friday nights there were always services and a lot of singing during and after dinner. Saturday we had special activities after services and after Havdallah (the evening prayer concluding Shabat) there were

Regina Wachner, Regina Miller, Sigmund and Hella Salz, Benjamin Wachner (Germany, 1933)

entertainers who put on puppet theater or led us in songs and dances. Once a week, those children whose parents had access to telephones were permitted to speak to their families. I looked forward to these telephone visits and often cried afterwards. But never too long. There was always a pair of arms waiting and some special goodies to comfort me. I had an unlimited expense account and we would often go to the nearby Friesien town to shop for goodies and souvenirs. Towards the end of August I bought some very beautiful gifts to bring back home. I bought a diamond broach for my mother, a pearl tie pin for my father and a little pocket knife inlaid with mother-of-pearl for my brother. These were real jewels, not costume jewelry. It was hard for my parents to cover up the shock over these gifts. They were in very good taste but very costly. However, seeing me fully recovered made it all worthwhile. Some time, much later, my mother tried to teach me how to shop and be aware of the cost of my purchases. I have no memory of harsh words from either of my parents. Was I a spoiled child? Probably. My memory is of total acceptance and approval. I have no memory of my parents ever fighting or yelling at one another. I am sure they had some disagreements but none that affected us. I clearly remember storming into my parent's bedroom one morning after a fight with Benno. My parents were still in bed, facing each other and holding hands. I stopped short and before I had a chance to complain, was invited to join them and that was what I did, forgetting all my problems. It was such a comforting feeling and is stored deeply in the vault of my memory.

Every Friday night there were fresh flowers brought home by my father or sent from the florist during his travels. My mother's disposition was often pensive and yet cheerful with us. Much later I learned that she had often been homesick living so far away from her family.

Children who feel loved seldom get into trouble. Oh, Benno and I did fight. I bothered him when he wanted to read and he in turn teased me telling me that I was just a stupid girl who should read more. It was never serious even though we yelled at each other. There were times when we both disobeyed our parents but never ever was there any corporal punishment. One day Benno and I were playing on the balcony. We got a box of chocolates, they were called cat's tongues (Katzen Zungen), and since they had been on the balcony table in the sun for quite a while they were melted. We smeared our faces with these chocolates leaving only our eyes and lips uncovered. Then we stood on chairs and started making noises and funny faces down at the passers-by. People looked up and laughed and before we knew it there was a crowd. A policeman came and told us to get off the chairs, we could topple over the balcony, he warned. Just then our mother, we called her Mutti, arrived from the store and I still remember her face. She came running up the stairs but by then we had gotten off the chairs and were licking each others faces to remove the chocolate. First she scolded the maid for not watching us and then came out after us. Well, we must have been a sight. She looked angry at first but then she started to laugh. She laughed so hard that the tears were rolling

Joseph Lobel and Gunther Salz

down her cheeks and she sat down on the floor and we next to her still licking the chocolate.

My mother had a younger sister, Tante Hella, who was married to Uncle Siegmund Salz and lived in Berlin as well. They had two children, Gunther and Irene.

Uncle Solomon Lobel, my mother's brother and his wife, Tante Fannie, also lived in Berlin. They had four children, Leo, Gerda (Warda), Eli and Doerchen (Dvora).

There was also my mother's other brother, Uncle Josef Lobel. He was the closest in age to my mother, only one year older. He was the only bachelor in the family and very often stayed with us when my father was away on business. I liked him a lot. He suffered from severe asthma and was very influential in the decision to send me to the sanatorium at such a young age to opt for a cure.

Then there was my mother's cousin whom we addressed as Tante. Her name was Regina (nee Schlanger) and she was married to Uncle Max Schneiderman. They had two children, Edith and Benjamin.

Every holiday, religious or secular, the families were together. Holidays were always special and made the wait for the summer vacations seem shorter when we would all gather in Brzostek, Poland, for visits with grandparents and all the other aunts and uncles. I have NO bad memories from my very early childhood.

Both my parents were born in Poland. My father, Jehoshua, was the oldest son in his family of nine children. His father was a Schochet (ritual slaughterer) in the little town of Ranizow, which was located about 40 kilometers from Rzeszow. He was regarded with much respect for his learning and the fact that he was a Cohen, a descendant of the tribe of Aaron, the high priest during the time of Moses. My grandfather's name was Aaron Wachner. He was tall and stately with a long beard and peyot. He had a full head of hair and bushy eyebrows under which were brown eyes that would sparkle with humor or become fierce when he disapproved of something. I liked him very much and remember sitting on his lap, pulling his beard and he would make believe that he was sleeping and snore to beat the band. Then he would catch my fingers in his mouth and I would squeal with delight. There were also some strange moments when we would visit. Grandfather never spoke directly to my father. I was a young child and could not understand but I never questioned. I accepted it as one more strange thing in a world that was so very different from the one I knew in Berlin. When I asked Benno about it he would shrug and say, "They are just different." I will talk more about that later.

Grandmother Gitel was short and very spry. Unfortunately, I do not know her maiden name. I remember walking with her to the forest to pick wild berries. On the way home she always took a shortcut and jumped over the fence with me in tow. When we came to visit she expressed her dismay at the way I looked and blamed my mother for not feeding me the right food. She called me "a langer loksch" (long noodle) and would prepare all kinds of food. Fresh berries and cream with lots of sugar, pancakes made of vegetables, little chicken livers which she fried in chicken fat and which I even then had trouble eating. But, since I loved her very much I would eat and often throw up afterwards. Grandmother was convinced that my mother did not know how to take care of children (even though my brother was chubby) since my mother too was very thin. Being thin in those days meant that you were not well.

My father had eight siblings. All but one were married and had children. Unfortunately. I do not remember all their names. We spent only two weeks every summer in Ranizow and the aunts and uncles were not always around. The names I do remember were, Uncle Moses, Uncle Itzchak, Uncle Leib, Aunt Sara, Aunt Miriam and the youngest, Aunt Channa. I believe all but Channa were married and had children but I do not remember them. Our visits were too short. Channa was living at home so I remember her best. She did not speak German (my mother tongue) but she spoke Yiddish and we got along very well. I liked her a lot. She had a pronounced limp and my mother told us that it was from an accident at birth. It is hard to believe that not one member of that family has survived.

My mother Regina (Rifka Lobel) was born in the small town of Brzostek. It is located between Tarnow and Jaslo, has its own municipality (court and jail), and a school run by the Catholic church. Many of the Jewish children in town attended this school. My mother and all of her siblings did. There was, of course, the Cheder (Hebrew school), which was attended by boys only. Girls learned to read and write and about tradition, religion and commandments at home. My mother was one of ten children. The oldest, Aaron and Benjamin (twins), died during World War I of influenza. Then there was Tante Hania, Uncle Berel, Uncle Solomon, Uncle Josef, my mother, Rifka, Tante Hella (Chaja), Tante Reisel and Tante Rondzia. Tante Hania was married and had five children. I do not remember their names or the name of her husband. They lived in Rzeszow and we usually saw them when we went to visit my paternal grandparents. Tante Hania had influenza during her first pregnancy and her son was born deaf. She had three daughters and another son. I liked visiting with Tante Hania. She was very pretty, had a lovely smile and was always very kind to me. She would shower Benno and me with kisses and gifts and little cakes and chocolate. I liked her a lot.

Uncle Berel Lobel was married to Tante Chava. She was extremely orthodox and they had 13 children. They lived in Dembica. We all went to their daughter Zelda's wedding. I must have been nine years old at the time. Zelda was a rare beauty. She had jet-black hair and green-blue eyes. She was tall and graceful and when we visited I often slept with her. My mother was very upset when she learned that Zelda would have to have her head shaved in the orthodox tradition. Tante Chava told my mother in no uncertain terms to "butt out." In the winter of 1940-1941 Zelda and her family were deported in cattle cars. She was seven months pregnant and gave birth in the cattle car. The baby died and Zelda bled to death. Their bodies were dumped from the moving train. Many years later Uncle Solomon told me that he met a neighbor of Uncle Berel and this man told him about the death of uncle Berel. On Simchat Torah all the Jewish men who were still in Dembica were rounded up, given Torahs and then made to dance with the Torahs in the middle of the square. This went on endlessly and many fell to the ground and were then shot. Uncle Berel was one of the last ones to die clutching the Torah. The bodies were dumped into a mass grave, set on fire and buried.

Grandfather Bzalel Lobel owned a store with building material and all iron, steel and metal supplies for house building. By the standards of that time he was considered a wealthy man. My grandparents owned a large house in the center of the square with four bedrooms. My grandparents' bedroom set was of cherry and mahogany, the bedspread and drapes were of dark green velvet trimmed with lace. Then there were two kitchens, a large storage room, a permanent Sukkah in the back which had a retractable roof and in back of that a vegetable garden and an orchard of fruit trees. There was a dining room for Shabbat and special holiday meals. There was a very large table, which easily seated 12 people, and a beautiful Persian carpet on the polished wood floor. In the main very large kitchen we ate most of our meals during the week. There was a window in that kitchen which looked out into an ally. On that window sill there was an ink bottle with a quill. Grandfather would sit there every Sunday and do his business accounts. When we lived in Berlin, Grandmother would write letters to us (in Yiddish) with that quill. I loved hearing her description of things that happened in our absence. The news was usually about people who died, who got married, who had a baby and who left town. The front of the house facing the square was occupied by the store. Grandfather ran the store and yet made time early morning of every day to study a page of Torah after the Schachrit (morning) service. His demeanor was serious but kind and always very loving to us. I never ever saw him angry. His customers, Jews and Gentiles, treated him with great respect. I learned much later that he would extend credit to many people and would always be repaid (sometimes in goods rather then money) and was much respected for that.

My Grandmother Rude (nee Schlanger) was tall, stately and known in town as the "healer." She knew a lot about herbal remedies and was much in demand by the local midwife. Often even the doctor would send people to her for treatment. She had a pantry filled with herbs drying on shelves; jars filled with herbs and fruits and also a big container with leaches. There was a shelf on which she kept peasant bread sliced thin which she would sprinkle with something and let mold grow on the bread. Frequently during our summer visits when we fell and scraped our knees and elbows, Grandmother would wash our wounds with one of her solutions (I think it was chamomile which she believed to be very healing), then take a piece of the dark moldy bread and tie it around our wounds. We never had infections. I had a wart on my left pinky. Mother got all kinds of salves and medicine for it in Berlin but it always came back. One day Grandmother took a small green (unripe) apple, cut it into pieces and kept rubbing it on my wart three or four times a day. After about a week the wart fell off and never came back. Some years later we learned that the origin of penicillin comes from a form of mold and today, acids are used to remove warts. There were times when people would come to her for cupping, which she administered expertly. Grandmother learned these remedies from her mother and grandmother. She often told me that she would have liked one of her daughters to learn from her but they were "too worldly." I, on the other hand, adored her and was a very willing student. My greatest pleasure was to sleep with Grandmother in the big bed in the kitchen. I would be put to bed in the bedroom and later at night, when everyone got ready for bed, Grandpa would carry me to the big bed. All her children were born in this bed and I still remember the smell of the fresh hay and how I used to curl into her body. How safe it felt, the closest thing to being in the womb. Many mornings Grandmother woke me at the crack of dawn. The roosters were crowing, birds chirping and the sky was covered in pink. Come child, she would say, we are going to find some herbs. She would pin up her skirts with a clothespin and barefoot we would go to the fields to gather what she needed. She would point out the different leaves, roots and herbs that grew wild and would tell me what they were for. Some to help women conceive, some to help with stomach problems, some for cleansing wounds and some awful smelling ones (I think they were a form of fungus) for poultices. My favorite ones were wild chamomile and peppermint. To this day I love tea from these herbs. Then, with our bags full we would take the long way back home and stop at my Aunt Rondzia (nee Lobel) and Uncle Julek Tintenfass's farm to get fresh milk straight from the morning milking, which she would make me drink bribed with a chocolate bar. I hated the milk but I would never oppose her in any way. What Grandmother did not know was that I was a highly allergic child. I suffered from hay fever (exacerbated by the mattress) and was allergic to the milk and chocolate. During the months which I spent at the sanatorium my grandmother was very upset. She truly believed that she could have found a way to heal me. In this respect of course she was wrong. When I returned the following summer I no longer slept in her bed and fresh milk from cows was forbidden. I had to keep a diet supervised by my mother and there were quite often serious disagreements between my mother and my grandmother. But ultimately Grandmother realized that I was getting healthier and she relented. I cannot remember bad feelings that would last during our visits. There were always so many aunts and uncles and cousins around that time just flew by. All my grandparents' siblings (Lobel and Schlanger families) lived either around the town square or nearby.

Our grandparents' house was quite large but not large enough to accommodate all the family with their spouses and offspring. So, when everyone came to visit at the same time, we were divided up to stay with my mother's aunts and uncles. We, my family, always stayed with Fetter (uncle) Elle Bergman. He had been married to my grandmother's sister. She died in childbirth at a very young age leaving behind a son Abe (Avrum) who as an adult emigrated to America. I met him years later when I came to America.

Fetter Elle had a large house and a shoe store in front of the house. My mother was his favorite niece (she was named after his wife) and we had a standing invitation to stay with him during our vacation. It was a stone's throw away from Grandmother so it never seemed that we were separated. Even though we stayed with him, I rarely slept there, opting to sleep with Grandmother. Saturday mornings all the men would leave for synagogue. Grandpa wore his long satin kittle (coat) and "shtrahmel" (round hat trimmed with mink tails). My father and most of the uncles wore modern clothing. After about an hour or so, Grandmother would gather all of us dressed in our best dresses and shoes and we would all go to synagogue. Grandmother Rude had two sheytels (wigs): one for everyday, and one for special holidays and the Shabbats when we were all together. The special one had a little adornment in it. It was studded with diamonds and rubies and when she wore it she seemed very regal to us children. She would gather her fringed paisley shawl around her and with a sweep would tell us all to follow her. When we got to temple the women would look at her and often say, "Oh, here goes Rude with her jewels." Grandma would smile with great dignity, point to us and say "THESE are my jewels, not the ones on my head." It was indeed a special time. We never spent much time inside the synagogue, by the time we got settled prayers would be almost finished and we would all walk home. We were a large group and I felt very important.

I met Tuska Schmidt in Brzostek when I was about six years old. She had lost her father (Josef) when she was three years old and her mother remarried a wealthy merchant who was widowed and had three children. His name was Fishel Goldman. Tuska (Taube) and her brother Genek (Gershon) came to live there when she was only six years old. We did not speak the same language but we played together and got along very well. I shall talk more about Tuska, Brzostek and my life there later.

In Berlin, when you entered the house in the winter there was always the comforting smell from the fireplace in the "Herrenzimmer." It was the main sitting room in the center of our apartment. The room had a large door (half glass), which led out onto a balcony facing Kantstrasse that was a wide avenue lined with linden trees. The street starts at Kurfurstendam and leads all the way up to Schloss Charlottenburg, which that section is named for. In the winter the large doors were closed and only the bare branches from the big trees could be seen through the sheer curtains. From spring through fall, on warm days the doors were kept open and the trees offered shade and one could hear the rustling of leaves from our balcony and from the interior of the apartment. Comforting sounds. There was an upholstered rocking chair and footstool in front of the fireplace. When Benno and I came home with our nanny (Kinder Madchen) from afternoon walks or ice skating, our cheeks aglow from the cold, we would run into the room where we would always find our mother with her book or embroidery. We peeled off our clothing and then would hasten to tell her, competing for attention, about our excursions. Often we walked all the way to the garden of the Schloss (castle) where we gathered leaves of particularly pretty colors and shapes, or found pine cones that we could paint and collect in a basket next to the fireplace. There was a playground in back of the Schloss and we spent many happy hours there. Then we settled down and got our goodies. Hot chocolate milk topped with whipped cream or chocolate pudding or, on rare occasions, ice cream. Ice cream we could only get on warm days since there was no freezer in the apartment and it had to be bought on a daily basis and eaten at once. Then there was always rest time. Our mother was a wonderful storyteller. She talked about her childhood and all her family. Most of the family still lived in Poland. She loved to sing and taught me many Jewish folk tunes. Sometimes the stories were sad. We learned early on about pogroms, about our mother's cousin who was attacked and murdered by a Cossack who raided her little town. That was the reason why our mother and Tante Hella left Poland. They came to Vienna in 1918. Our mother was born September 1, 1899, and Tante Hella was just two years younger.

They were both very pretty and it was not safe for them to stay in Poland. Uncle Josef had gone to Vienna to escape from the army in 1915 or 1916. He became a partner and then sole owner of a pub where most Jewish Polish refugees gathered for food and company. When my mother and aunt came to Vienna they helped Uncle Josef in the pub and shortly after their arrival my mother met my father. They were married in Vienna in 1921 and moved to Berlin, Germany. Tante Hella met Uncle Siegmund and they also followed to Berlin.

At that time, even though Jews were never really wanted or accepted in Germany, it nevertheless was a haven for Jews. In Berlin synagogues flourished and presented a life of safety and comfort for most people. Jewish philosophers like Martin Buber, Franz Rosenzweig or Eric Fromm were much admired and people flocked to hear their lectures. It was the beginning of the reform movement in Judaism and the creation of the first reform synagogue in Berlin (the first one to be destroyed during Kristallnacht in 1938). Rabbi Samson Raphael Hirsch, an orthodox rabbi, realized that the time had come to make changes in orthodox tradition to accommodate a large segment of Jews who were brought up in ultra-orthodox families and needed to fit into the general German population. Change, perhaps even radical change, was necessary if orthodoxy was to survive. And so, Rabbi Hirsch founded Neo-Orthodoxy. Orthodox Jews shed their long coats (kittels), cut their beards and payot, and formed synagogues that continued to adhere strictly to basic laws with room for change from old Eastern European customs. He was the founder of the synagogue that we attended on Fasanenstrasse. The name Rabbi Hirsch was often heard in our household. Although Jews enjoyed this freedom they were never a part of government or policy making. Jews were on the outside of history making. Their only sense of belonging was through the synagogue.

I remember our afternoons of comfort and a feeling of safety. We would while away hours in front of the fireplace, sometimes fall asleep, dusk descended and we never bothered to light the lamps.

Then, always punctually at 4.30 pm., the doorbell would ring and break the spell. Our Hebrew tutor came four afternoons. Reluctantly we would give up our place in the cozy room and after our tutor finished his tea (served in a glass with a handle and cube sugar) we went to our room, which had a large round table, and got ready for our lessons. The tutor was a kind and infinitely patient and pious man. More often than I care to admit, I made faces in back of him that used to make Benno laugh and bring a frown to the face of the tutor. But he never scolded us. We learned Hebrew reading and writing and liked it best when he told stories from the Bible. He stayed for an hour, sometimes longer and afterwards (especially in winter) had more tea and sat and talked with our mother.

Is it possible that I have forgotten or possible there were no disturbing moments during those winter afternoons? If there were upsetting times, I do not remember them so they must have been meaningless to me. I loved those winters and almost 70 years later still remember the smells, tastes and sounds of that time. There are times when I am doing something and a smell will awaken a memory, which then becomes almost tangible. Our mother, Mutti, was a very sensitive person. She would make us aware of things surrounding us: long shadows from the branches bowing and bending in the wind outside the windows, the wind howling would tell a story of its own. There were no fears, only an awareness of silence or sound. The buzz of bees in the summer, the difference between the sound of a fly or that of a mosquito. Crickets in the evening had a song of their own. The persistent cooing of the turtle doves. When I was in Israel in 1977 (and four summers thereafter) I stayed on a kibbutz. I heard the cooing of turtle doves and it catapulted me back to my childhood. (In the midst of the political chaos in 1977 I could feel comfort.) Some of the sounds could predict changes in weather. The quiet before a storm. Many times we would wait on the balcony for thunder and lightning and then watch through the glass doors or windows. Ladybugs (Mai Kafer) were Mutti's favorite little bugs. Since I was born in May she would always decorate the birthday table with little chocolate ladybugs. These were covered in red tinfoil with little black dots. Lily of the valley (Mai Glockchen) was her favorite flower. The little white blossoms gave off a delicate fragrance and always found a place in the center of the birthday table. How lucky that she had the sensitivity and the time and patience to share all this with us. Snow in the winter looked different when it was very cold or when the sun hit the surface. Smells and tastes of various foods became a guessing game. Sometimes Mutti would blindfold us and we had to guess first by smell then by taste what was put in front of us. Thus we learned to taste all food and develop likes and dislikes. There was no television. We had a radio but it was for music or special news reports. So, we read or were read to. Mutti loved to sing. She taught me many Yiddish songs from her own childhood. I learned a song about Yente Dvoshe's Homantaschen around Purim time. I learned My Yiddishe Mamme and often Mutti would cry when she and I sang it. She missed her mother and the life she had at home surrounded by brothers and sisters, aunts, uncles and cousins. There were so many of them. There was a song she sang from a play. "It might be that I will never reach my goal; It might be that my God does not even exist; In dreams I am happy and the world is bright: In dreams the sky is bluer then blue." I did not understand it but I liked the way she sang it and remember it still. Also a song about a white goat and a little boy in the cradle: he will sell raisins and almonds and that will be his profession. "Rojinkes mit Mandeln." When we went to Brzostek I would perform for my grandparents. We lived sheltered lives; our minds were given a chance to wander and fantasize. I have many happy memories.

Then, twice a year the dressmaker would "invade" the house. She came with pamphlets of the latest fashions, swatches of material and Mutti and I would pick out the clothing to be made for the forthcoming season. I loved to do this and felt very special. Tante Fanni used to tell Mutti to have certain things that were made for me also made for Gerda. We were both the same size. Many years later I learned that Warda (then Gerda) resented this very much. The dressmaker would stay for about two weeks in a room in the back of the apartment, which was called the office. It was a fun time and I loved watching her and learned a lot about her relationship with my mother. They were close friends of a number of years. I don't know what happened to her.

Our father traveled a lot and the times when he was home were very special. We took part in the preparations of favorite food and cakes. Our father was a major importer of oriental rugs. He always came home with exotic gifts from Persia, dolls (I had a collection of dolls from many countries) and hand-carved items from Holland or the Baltic Sea. He told stories of various customs and foods. Since he never ate any non-kosher food he would tell us about finding his way to kosher homes (there were no kosher restaurants) or sometimes eat nothing but fruit that could be peeled. But Pappi was always home for major holidays and sometimes even for Purim or Chanukah. That was the time for dinner parties, family visits and for us to show what we learned in his absence. It was also time for special excursions. Both our parents loved opera. The first time we, Benno and I, were taken to the opera (*La Boheme*) I was eight years old. I cried at the end and Benno (macho man) called me a sissy. He knew it was all make-believe; after all, Mimi got up for bows when it ended.

When Pappi was home it was also a time for special tasks. Benno had his tonsils removed and I had a tooth extracted. Mutti had surgery on one of her legs but I do not remember what it was for. She had to stay in bed for a while and Pappi took over directing the household. I remember that he would put on an apron and make meals for us when the maid was off. He tried to tell us stories and they were always funny and we laughed a lot. He had a great sense of humor and I have no memory from that time of him ever frowning or being angry. I was born with scoliosis of the spine and had to do special exercises. I had to crawl on my hands and knees for ten minutes twice daily. I did not like that routine and so Pappi and Benno joined in and it became a family game. We had races around the room and somehow I always won. Of course Mutti was the judge.

Friday nights and Saturday mornings we all went to temple. Even when Pappi was away. Pappi was a Cohen (like his father before him) and always received special Kavod (honor) in the great synagogue on Fasanenstrasse. Pappi was a Baal Torah (one who is proficient in reading the Torah) and loved to read the Torah on Saturday mornings. When he was home he often shared the Bima (stage) with the cantor or other Baale Torah. The temple on Fasanenstrasse was beautiful and just a few block from our home.

When I was back in Berlin in 1990 (by special invitation from the German government) I found only one column and some old pictures of that great synagogue. I was heartsick, walked around with a lump in my throat and could not wait to leave. It is really all gone! Some years back Dennis Waldman introduced a new nigun (melody) to the choir. It is to the words "Havein Yakir Li." Suddenly the memory of my father chanting this particular part of the high holiday prayer came alive. Father was standing on the Bima with the Cantor, wearing his white Kittel (gown) and large Tallith (prayer shawl), which he wrapped around Benno while holding him by the shoulders. My mother and I were sitting upstairs in the women's section and when I asked her what Pappi was doing she told me that the words mean "My son my beloved" and Pappi was singing it to Benno. I love this nigun and yet it evokes such painful memories.

Pesach was an especially festive time. Rosenthal dishes came down in boxes from the storage room in the attic of the apartment house. The whole apartment got scrubbed, carpets were cleaned and not a crumb of food or dust was left in any corner. The kitchen was last. The lovely hand-painted dishes, each piece a slightly different design, the crystal goblets and platters were washed and all the silver got polished. The large dining room table (it accommodated 16 people) sparkled and glowed with all the finery kept especially for Pesach. And all those smells and sounds from the kitchen! Mutti always hired extra help and she was busy for days with preparations. She supervised all the cooking and baking and the pantry was filled with goodies for the holidays. There was little or no time for storytelling. I loved "helping" in the kitchen and Benno especially liked tasting and giving his stamp of approval.

By late afternoon of the first Seder guests would arrive. Tante Hella and Uncle Siegmund with Gunther and Irene (little Renie). Uncle Joseph, the only bachelor in the family, and my mother's cousin Schmuel Schlanger. Some years after the war I established contact with him in London, England. He was married to an orthodox woman and they have four children. Then came Uncle Moses, my father's brother whose wife and children went home to Poland to her family for holidays so he came alone. He had my father's sense of humor and we loved him dearly. Uncle Moses was a partner and in charge of warehouses in my father's business. Benno and I, Gunther and Renie loved these holidays. We had new clothing and new shoes and were all allowed to stay up late and always watched carefully for the coming of the Messiah. Benno, being the oldest, had to open the doors wide and the cup filled with wine in the center of the table always trembled. Pappi and Uncle Moses would secretly shake the table but we children were convinced that the Messiah was there albeit invisible. I do not remember ever finishing an entire Seder. It went on for many hours and having been given some wine and the late hour, Renie, Gunther and I usually would fall asleep in our chairs and be put to bed. Gunther and Renie stayed over night and in the morning we all had Matzebrei for breakfast. These are the memories I cling to, especially on Pesach when other more terrible memories begin to crowd in.

Uncle Solomon and Tante Fannie with Leo, Gerda (now Warda), Eli and Dvora also lived in Berlin. They did not live within walking distance so the holidays that did not permit travel were not spent together. But we saw them very frequently. On all outings to Wahnsee, Grunewald, the big zoo or the playground at Schloss Charlottenburg we were together. Leo, being the oldest, was always in charge of the rest of us. Tante Fannie, Tante Hella and Mutti would spend time talking and just seemed to enjoy being together. We children loved these outings. I remember one time when we were in Grunewald we had a water drinking contest. The winner of the game was the one who could drink the most water. The outcome was that we, the younger ones threw up and little Dvora (she was the youngest) and Renie would pee in their pants. You can imagine that that did not sit well with the mothers. Then one day we had gone to Wahnsee to the beach. Eli and Benno, both mischievous, buried all the mothers' shoes and when the time came to go home it took a long time to find them. They found all but one of Mutti's sandals. At first Mutti was very angry and promised to punish Benno when we got home, but then the comedy of the situation took hold and we all laughed (including Mutti) all the way home. She had to go barefoot on the tramway and then home. It was not exactly her style. Tante Fannie was ready to kill Eli but he ran away from her. I do remember that afternoon clearly with some fright but mostly with laughter.

My mother's cousin, Tante Gina (Regina), was married to Uncle Max. They had two children, Edith and Ben. Uncle Max was a furrier and they lived some distance from us. We visited with them often but rarely spent religious holidays together. Uncle Max did not come from an orthodox home and they did not go to temple. I liked Tante Gina very much and looked forward to visits with them. She was not a happy person even then and often we would see our mother sitting with her and Tante Gina would cry. Edith was a beautiful child but not a happy child. She was the "cry baby" in the group and because of that was often excluded from our games. Kids can be cruel. I liked her a lot and often just stayed with her and played with her dolls. Some of these memories are foggy. I think children shut out and suppress painful experiences. And then there was Hella Schmerling, who was a very good friend of Mutti and Tante Hella. I don't remember her husband's name but they had a son Hans. They lived in the apartment next to Tante Hella and I was often told that Hans and I were the exact same age. When the families would visit we were both put in the same crib. I saw Hella Schmerling in 1967 in Israel. She lived in

Kiriat Bialik outside of Tel Aviv. Hans is now called Chaim Shamur. I visited Hella Schmerling in 1978. She was then living in an assisted living dwelling. It was her birthday and when I wished her happy birthday in Hebrew she corrected me. My wish for her was to live to 100 AND 20 but she said the wish should be to live to 100 LIKE 20. It was a play on words. Not long after, Hella died and sadly I have lost all contact with Chaim. That was the inner circle of my family in Berlin.

This comfortable carefree life lasted until about 1933. That is when we would hear radio broadcasts of Hitler's speeches. There was much discussion by the adults and it filtered through to us. Benno and I would watch the Hitler youth with lit torches march on the big avenue in front of our house and it all looked so exiting. I thought Benno was jealous that he could not march with them. As time went on we noticed that the children who we used to ice skate with would no longer include us in their games nor invite us to their homes. At first we could not understand but then our parents explained it to us. That was when I first became aware of the word "anti-Semitism." I was about nine years old. The winter of 1935-1936 was filled with tension. Our afternoons were no longer as peaceful. The tutor left Germany and no one was there to replace him for us. My father traveled less and there were many serious discussions between him and the uncles. I cannot remember the exact words but the topic was about getting out of Germany. Uncle Josef tried to persuade my parents to leave Europe but neither would hear of leaving all the family behind. The hope was that this atmosphere would pass. After all, the Germans were the most civilized people. Surely they would come to their senses and get rid of that mad man. Uncle Josef had read *Mein Kampf* and he was of the opinion that Jews were no longer safe in Germany. Where could we go? Poland was known for its anti-Semitism, but Uncle Josef wanted us out while we could still go. My father called him a pessimist and their discussions were often quite heated. Benno and I would huddle in our beds, listen and worry. We loved both our father and Uncle Josef, but who was right? No longer did we stay at the window and watch the Hitler youth march. I remember falling asleep in the evening and being awakened by the marching in front of our window. They marched with lit torches, sang songs and stepped with great precision in their boots. That must have made a very strong and lasting impression on me. Marching boots (which were repeated later on) are in my nightmares even today.

In March of 1936 my father was approached by one of his employees who demanded that he hand over the business to him. My father ignored the demand and fired him. Two weeks later, as my father was leaving for Elbing (to one of the warehouses) he was arrested at the train station. He was taken to SS headquarters in Berlin, Ploetzensee, interrogated, brutally beaten and sent to the concentration camp Dachau. No one knew anything about it. Then one day a package arrived addressed to me. That was not unusual since our father would often send packages for either Benno or me. This, however, was different. We opened the package, which had no return address, and to our horror found my father's blood-soaked clothing with a note attached "Juden raus" (Jews get out). We realized that something had happened to him and that he would not be home for Pesach. Uncle Josef and Uncle Solomon instituted a search and found out that our father was arrested as a "political alien." The nature of his punishment or the length of his incarceration at Dachau was not known. Some weeks later an SS man (special division appointed to deal with the "Jewish" problem) came to our house and handed my mother an eviction notice. We were to leave Germany within 48 hours and take only what we could carry with us. We began to weed out things, gave some items to neighbors and started packing the most important items which we could hand carry. On May 2, 1936, under the supervision and scrutiny of the SS, we left our apartment and were escorted to a train for Poland. The apartment was locked up and no one was allowed to enter it again. Prudently, my mother had given a duplicate set of keys to our neighbor (a German woman) who was appalled at what was happening to us. That proved to be very advantageous later on.

Previous train rides to Poland were always full of excitement. It took close to twenty hours by train from Berlin to Tarnow and we always had our own compartment. Benno and I loved these train rides and Pappi used to have an atlas and point out where we were going and where we were at given moments. There was a dining car attached to the train and we ate dinner and breakfast elegantly served. Then there was the excitement of crossing the border. The border police came to our compartment to check our passports. They were always very polite. Then, from Tarnow to Brzostek was about 45 km. which we traveled by horse and buggy.

This trip in 1936 was very different. We were without Pappi and we did not have our own compartment. We were sitting on hard benches and barely slept during the night. We were not allowed into the dining car and had to make do with some cold sandwiches. When we got to the border we had to get off the train and go to an office at the station. Mother was questioned at length and it seemed to take forever to get our passports cleared. The atmosphere was frightening. We went as far as Katowice where Tante Rondzia and her husband Uncle Julek Tintenfass lived. They met us at the train station and we came to their small apartment. Everything was so different, new and strange. Their apartment consisted of a large living /dining room and one bedroom. There was a small kitchen and the toilet was out in the hall and was shared by three families. There was no tub for bathing and no running hot water. Quite a culture shock for us.

Tante Rondzia welcomed us with open arms and somehow we all fit into that small space. Mutti and I slept on a couch in the living room and Benno on the floor next to us. A few days later Uncle Josef arrived and the effort to free our father began. In June we all went to Brzostek (Tante Rondzia and Uncle Julek owned a farm there) and life took on a more normal shape for us children. Twice during the summer Mutti went to Katowice to try and get a visa to go back to Germany to retrieve some of our belongings. We came back to Katowice after Sukkot and soon after Mother went back to Germany with Uncle Josef. She was his favorite sister and he was always there for her and all of us. While Mutti was away I got sick. When I first got sick I did not tell my aunt. I was determined to wait for Mother to return. Benno was in cohoots with me and whenever Tante Rondzia was out shopping (a daily routine since there was no refrigeration) he would feed me aspirins. The day Mutti came back from Germany we met her at the train station with flowers. As soon as she saw me she knew something was wrong. She took me in her arms felt my head and I started to cry and collapsed. I ran a very high fever and have only fragmented memory of that time. It turned out to be a severe kidney infection (nephritis), which lasted through the winter. Around Chanukah time my father was released and came home to us. He looked different, the sparkle in his eyes was not there and only much later I found out that he had many festering wounds on his back from his incarceration in Dachau. No longer were we the carefree children. Although our parents shielded us from the horrors of our father's experiences, we were keenly aware of the change in our parents' demeanor. Since I was still sick, much of that time is a blur in my memory.

Within a few weeks after Pappi came home, we moved to a large apartment in a brand-new house in a very nice section of Katovice near a large park. The building was new with ultramodern appliances, hot and cold running water, and a bathroom with a sunken bathtub. Mutti had to lay flat on her stomach to wash our hair but after having lived with Tante Rondzia without any amenities this was a minor problem. The apartment was very spacious and Benno and I no longer shared a bedroom. Our address was Ulica Stalmacha 26. There was a courtyard surrounded by three buildings and in the center there were lovely flowers and benches. Little children could play and ride their bicycles in the courtyard. Since we moved in the winter we did not see this until the spring and it was a nice surprise. Many

Regina and Jehoshua Wachner (Poland, 1937)

years later, Uncle Solomon told me that my father was co-owner of this apartment complex. Obviously, I have no papers to confirm this. When my mother had gone back to Berlin she was able to get most of our furniture out of the apartment and have it shipped to Katovice. This was done with the help of the neighbor who had the keys and told the authorities that she wanted all the furniture for her niece who lived in Poland for "Volksdeutsche" (Germans who worked and lived in Poland). She was a very fine person and I have no idea what happened to her. With all our belongings in place we began to feel more at home.

Benno and I had private tutors to learn the Polish language and to continue with our Hebrew lessons. Many were the times that I was too sick to learn and as a result I missed a full year of school. Benno enrolled in mid-session at a nearby public school which was not much to his liking. He was a very bright boy and soon caught up with the other students. There was overt anti-Semitism since the school was supervised and much influenced by the Catholic church. Jews were considered Christ killers and most Jewish children suffered attacks from their classmates to which the teachers kept their eyes closed.

My father had some contacts with people and within a few months opened a store on Ulica 3 Maia. The store had radios, bicycles and ready-made clothing for men, women and children. In those days, most people did not buy ready-made clothing. Those who could afford it had clothing made to order and the poorer people made their own. My father's store provided all these things and it was the first store of its kind where people could purchase goods and pay for them over time. The name of the store was "Dom Ratalny" (the house of credit). It became an instant success. There was a man who managed the radio section. He was called by us "Mr. Engineer" and was in charge of assembly and repairs. He was very kind to us but particularly to Benno, who loved watching him. Mr. Engineer taught Benno the game of chess. Benno loved it and soon became very proficient. In December 1938 Benno entered a contest (encouraged by Mr. Engineer) with students at the Bendzin University and he won a prize. The prize was a chess board made of marble and the chess pieces were carved of ivory.

My father also became the representative of Suchard Chocolate of Switzerland. Much later, Uncle Solomon told me that my father had all profits deposited in a bank in Switzerland. In 1966 Uncle Solomon went to Switzerland and tried to find the account in a bank (I have no idea which one) but he was told that there was no such account. We now know that most documents were shredded soon after the war. I still have a claim pending.

Sometime during the early spring of 1937 I finally got better and my mother took me to Brzostek. I stayed with my grandparents and by the time Benno and my mother joined me in July I was fully recovered. Tuska lived in a large house across from my grandparents. There was an attic in the house and we used to climb up to the attic and invent games. There were some roof tiles and Tuska would bring up some food and we used the tiles as plates. There was a time when Tuska's mother was looking for us. She kept calling and we did not respond. We were hiding for no good reason and giggled until we were finally found. I also remember that whenever it rained Tuska would come out of the house, wave to me across the town square and I would come running and the two of us would go walking in the rain singing and laughing. These were summer showers and we would get soaked and sometimes scolded by our mothers. Every Saturday afternoon the family would rest. Tuska and I would go for walks. We went through fields or sometimes to the nearby woods where we feasted on berries. Sometimes we took off our shoes and waded in the brook. Once I slipped and fell in the water. My beautiful Shabbos dress (light blue wool with a full skirt and embroidered collar and cuffs) got wet. We sat for a long time in the sun but eventually I had to go home wet and deal with the disapproval of my parents and grandparents. But we had fun, laughed a lot and it was worth it. Thus a bond was created between the two of us. My language skills improved although I never lost my accent.

My father's business flourished. In the winter 1938 we went by car to Zakopane, which is a ski resort town in the Carpathian Mountains. We stayed in a kosher hotel and both Benno and I learned to ski. We had our own little cabin but had our meals in the dining room of the main house. When we were not out skiing, we went sleigh riding in a horse drawn sled. It was a lot of fun and my parents had many friends with whom they spent their evenings. There were daily services at the hotel and Shabbos was very special and restful. We used to read a lot and I do not remember ever being bored.

I hated to go back because I did not like school. There was overt anti-Semitism and I was scared of some of the children who taunted us. The teachers closed their eyes and never came to our rescue. Benno and I walked home together and often we had to run to escape the stones which were thrown at us. Benno began to train me to become the fastest runner and he would time me. Faster, faster he would yell, they are coming, even when there was no one around. I did become a very fast runner but was still afraid. In the winter we would take our skis to school but that lasted for only a short time. Our ski poles were stolen and after two such incidents we gave up. Benno did very well in school and I just about made passing grades. Most of the time I was unhappy and dreaded any tests. Children made fun of my accent and I made no friends in school.

I used to love Friday afternoons. As soon as we came home from school I would rush to change and go ice skating with friends. These were friends from Bnei Akiba, a Zionist organization to which I, like most Jewish children, belonged. Benno belonged to Beitar, which had a different philosophy. Bnei Akiba believed that peace can be achieved without fighting, just with words. Beitar believed that we had to learn to defend ourselves with any means possible.

Then one Friday at the end of February, I was particularly anxious to go skating. I had been in the house for two weeks with bronchitis and this was the first week I was back in school. I could not wait to go with my friends. Mutti was home with Pani Rosa (Mrs. Rosa) who came every Friday afternoon to give Mutti a manicure, pedicure and massage. Mutti did not want me to go skating since I had been sick and the weather was very cold. Also, you will be late for candle lighting, she said. I did not listen and when Pani Rosa was busy giving her the massage I snuck out of the house. It was just great at the ice skating rink. The music was playing and all my friends were there. My friends and I made a chain (snake) and we skated with great speed. The last one would get whipped around the corner and then become the head of the chain. This way we took turns and every one had a chance to be the tail end. It was great fun. That fateful Friday afternoon, while I was the tail, I had a head-on collision with a boy much bigger than myself. We crashed and I fell backwards, landed on my right wrist and it broke in two places. I was picked up by the first aid people who put on a bandage and wanted to escort me home. I told them to take me to the store. I knew Benno and Pappi would be at the store before temple and since I had disobeyed my mother I did not want to face her alone. When I got to the store they were not yet there but Mr. Engineer was there and I waited with him. I was in great pain and felt very guilty for not listening to my mother.

When Pappi and Benno came I started to cry and told them that I had been punished for disobeying Mutti. Pappi never said a word. When we came home Mutti called out from the dining room asking if I was with them. Pappi went to her by himself and talked with her. I was never scolded but Mutti looked quite unhappy. I had a terrible night of pain and in the morning we went to the hospital and I had to have my arm set in a plaster cast that reached over the elbow.

March 12, 1938. Austria, by popular vote, became part of greater Germany.

March 15, 1938. Germans invade Czechoslovakia without any resistance.

It is Benno's birthday. He is 13 and becomes a Bar Mitzva. Our apartment has sliding doors that divide the salon (living room) and dining room. The doors are opened and the rooms are prepared for a sit-down kiddush dinner for 40 people. After temple we all come home, Benno delivers his Drosha (an interpretation of the parscha, chapter of the week) and after that dinner was served. It was very festive. My beautiful Bar Mitzva dress had to be altered to allow for the cast on my arm. I was cranky and I was jealous of Benno who was getting all the attention. My father, in his ultimate wisdom, told me that if I learn to read a chapter of the Book of Ruth (in Hebrew) by the time I am 13, I would have the same party as Benno. I did, and in 1939 after we came back from temple (it was Shavuot) I chanted the first chapter of the Book of Ruth to all the invited guests and then had the same kiddush dinner as Benno.

Anti-Semitism was nothing new to our parents. Germany, Hitler and his minions were far away and so we were lulled into a false sense of security. Not for long though.

November 9, 1938. Kristallnacht. We learn that temples all over Germany were destroyed, books and Torah scrolls burned, and store windows broken and stores shut down for good.

In the fall of 1937 Benno and I had joined the Zionist organizations, Betar and Bney Akiva. Betar was a militant organization determined to get back the land of Palestine. If not through negotiations they were ready to fight for it. Bney Akiva was the opposite. Not by strength and not by sword was our motto. Only by peaceful means and negotiations. We learned about Herzl and his dream of a Jewish homeland and at the tender age of 12 I read the book *Utopia, Alt Neuland* in which Herzl described the life in Palestine filled with Jews from all over the world. Benno and I were registered with Youth Alyah for possible emigration to Palestine. It was the answer to the feeling of insecurity in the Polish environment. There was political unrest and children in school were given gas masks that we had to carry with us at all times. We were being taught how to jump out of windows from the fourth floor into a sack-like funnel and were caught on the bottom in a net. It was frightening and I had nightmares about it for a long time. As I mentioned before, through our organizations we made friends with other Jewish children, went ice skating, on bicycle outings and overnight camping trips. That association kept our spirits high.

December 1938.

Tante Hella and Uncle Siegmund left Berlin with their children and came to Poland. My father,s closest friend, Herr Berger, was also of Polish origin. He had married a German Jewish lady. He left Berlin but his wife was not given an exit visa. After Kristallnach he somehow arranged to smuggle her across the border to join him in Poland. In retrospect that was not wise. Had she remained in Berlin she might have survived. I clearly remember the night when we were all in our dining room awaiting her arrival. The time she was to appear had long past and Herr Berger was pacing the floor and wringing his hands. At one point I walked over to him and told him not to worry, I know she will soon come I said. He embraced me and told me that he would give me a big donation for Keren Kayemet for Israel if that was true. She arrived a short while later almost frozen to death. The next day we learned that she had fallen into the river at the border crossing and almost drowned. Her guide rescued her and finally delivered her to our house. I got a large bank note (20 Zloty — about $20) for my blue box.

Early in the spring of 1939 Benno was registered in a school in London, England. He was to leave for that school on September 3, 1939.

In July 1939 I went to a camp that was to prepare us for life on a kibbutz. It was really quite rough and I remember having a hard time sleeping in tents and bathing in the ice-cold river. Before the end of the month I got sick with tonsillitis and after four days of high fever was sent home. I recuperated but not quite fully. We went to Brzosted for two weeks but had to get back to Katowitce to prepare for Benno's departure to the school in England. His trunks with all his belongings (even his prized chess set) were packed and shipped to England by the middle of August.

Around August 20 I again got sick and this time the fever did not subside. I had again a sore throat, my fever spiked and I was unable to move my limbs. The pain in my joints was severe and I was in and out of consciousness. I awoke one day to find an elderly gentlemen sitting next to my bed. He kept shaking his head and I heard him say, "…hopeless, we have no medication, she may last two weeks." My mother was sobbing and had to leave the room. I lost consciousness again and when I woke my brother was sitting next to my bed holding my hand. He told me that the man was a famous doctor from Warsaw who my father persuaded to come to examine me. His opinion was that I had either polio or rheumatic fever. Either I would be crippled by polio or my heart would not survive the rheumatic fever since it was already affected. Benno told me that he would always be with me and that Pappi had gone in search of medication for my heart (digitalis) and a nurse who could stay with us.

September 1, 1939.

We are awakened 5 o'clock on the morning of September 1, 1939, by wailing sirens. Both my parents and Benno are on the bed with me. I look at Mutti and say "Happy Birthday" and she starts to cry. "How did you know the date?" she asks. To this day I don't know how I knew. Moments later the bombs are falling all around us and Pappi is begging Mutti and Benno to go to the shelter. They refused and we all huddled on the big bed with covers over our heads. I was in terrible pain, had high fever and could not be moved. The windows were shattered, the building next to ours got a direct hit and our kitchen was in shambles. I am again unconscious. I am awakened when the son of my parents' closest friends is holding my hand and kissing it. "Malutka" (little one), he said. "I am leaving but we shall meet again. And then we shall never be separated. Get well for me and remember I will be back." He was almost seven years older and I had a crush on him. He was my first love and I am sure that he liked me very much. When he left I cried bitterly. His name was Zyga Steinhauer.

I have no conscious memory of the rest of the day. Saturday morning September 2, 1939, the militia came and took my father with his car into the army. He asked to be allowed to transport us out of Katowitze since I was so very ill. They refused.

Sunday, September 3, 1939. Benno is supposed to leave but all civilian trains are cancelled. In the early afternoon, Uncle Julek comes to our house and starts loading a large horse drawn wagon with some essential clothing, a mattress and bedding. I am lifted onto the wagon on the mattress and we leave our home. Road conditions were impossible to pass. The army had first right and then came people fleeing on foot with their meager belongings. Old people being transported in wheelbarrows holding babies in their arms. Bombs falling all around, panic, screams and no shelter. The horses reared and had to be controlled by hand. There was no room for Benno on the wagon and he rode his bicycle next to it. When the bombs were falling everyone who could fit took shelter under the wagon. Only my mother and I huddled on top. We arrive in Krakow in the late afternoon. Uncle Julek pulls up next to a hospital run by the Catholic church. My mother pleads with them to take me in. When I was not delirious I complained of constant pain, mostly in my chest and arms. The head nurse (a nun) of the hospital takes one look at me and tells my mother that there is no room for Jewish children. All the pleading and offers of money or jewels did not soften her heart. We left in the middle of another air raid. After some time we came to a little town on the outskirts of Krakow. Uncle Julek took the horses to a stream and allowed them to rest for a while. An old man approaches my mother and asks, "Di bist a Yidishe Tochter?" Are you a Jewish daughter? Why are you crying so bitterly? My mother points to me and tells him night is coming and we have no shelter. The next thing I know I am in a large warm bed being fed some chicken broth. This man, with only one room for himself and his wife, took us in and shared not only their only bed but the little food they had. He was a true Tzadik (righteous person) and deserved to go to heaven. Who knows when and how he and his wife died? The next day he went to Shachrit (morning service) with my uncle and my brother. When they came back he walked over to the bed, put his hands on my head and said that I was a blessed child. At services they were told that the hospital in Krakow, which was not far from the railroad station, received a direct hit and there were many casualties. My mother swore that she would never put me in a hospital. To her it was a sign from God.

September 4, 1939, we leave for Tarnow. My condition is worse. I cannot swallow and I cannot breathe lying down and cannot sit up on my own. My mother sits on the wagon holding me in her arms in an upright position. I have a dream that we are in a green pasture, the sun is shining and there is a field full of white geese. It is so peaceful and there is music playing in the distance. I look around and there is Pappi coming towards us smiling and holding out his hands. I run to him and I have no pain. He smiles and tells me that he always knew that I would be well again. I am awakened by screams. Bombs are falling in the distance and the horses are frightened and rear. The wagon is on a hill and the horses are pushing backwards. The back wheels are over an embankment and people are running to stop the wagon from going over the precipice. Benno puts his bicycle under the back wheels and we stop. The bicycle was crushed and Benno had to walk from then on. My mother looks at me, wondering why I am smiling. I tell her about my dream and she cries. From your lips to God's ears, she tells me. Late in the evening we arrive in Tarnov. Tante Hella lives there somewhere and Uncle Julek leaves us on the wagon and goes to find the address. There had been a number of bomb hits and passage with horse and wagon through narrow streets was impossible. My fever was raging and I have no recollection of time. It was dark and I was being carried by Uncle Julek upstairs and put to bed. Tante Hella's brother-in-law is a doctor who looks me over and shakes his head. "It is quite hopeless, I am afraid that her heart will not endure," he said. He tells my mother that he and his wife are leaving for Russia (she was pregnant) at night and gave us the name of a doctor friend of his who would look in on us.

My mother is sleeping and Tante Hella sits next to me with her head resting on the bed. I wake and ask her if I will die now. Benno who was sleeping on the floor next to my bed hears that and yells out, "No, not now, not for a long time." Tante Hella feeds me warm milk and little bits of chocolate (no worry about allergies) and tells me that I will recover and run and play again with little Renie. We will go to Brzostek and Grandma will make me well. I sleep the first peaceful sleep in days.

I am awakened to air raid sirens. Tante Hella, Gunther and Renie go to the shelter and want to take Benno with them. He refuses to leave us. I am dead weight and cannot be carried. Uncle Julek went back to Katowitze to salvage some of his belongings and Uncle Siegmund (Tante Hella's husband) had left with his brother and sister-in-law for Russia to escape the Polish army. So we stayed huddled on the bed with blankets to shield us from glass. Bombs were falling all around us and we received a direct hit. There was a chandelier over the bed that started swaying. It was going to crash. Benno climbed on the bed on top of me and Mutti put a blanket over all of us. The chandelier came down on his back but thanks to the heavy blankets Benno was not badly hurt. There was another hit and half of the building collapsed. The bed, which had been in the middle of the room, was now at the very edge of the building. Mutti climbed over me to the other side and looked to the stairwell. We were on the third floor and half of the stairs were gone. When the "all clear" sirens started, people came running out of shelters. Tante Hella stood at the bottom screaming for help to get us out. I am being lifted onto a ladder, tied to it with rope and lowered by human hands from one stairwell over a void to another until we reached bottom. Where to go? Benno had the address of the doctor who was supposed to look in on us. He made his way to her house and she took us all in. Another saint. She had a small apartment in back of her office where everyone found a place on the floor. The examining table in her office became my bed for the next two and a half months. She had some sulfur medication as well as digitalis for the heart and, best of all, aspirins. Against all expectations I began to recover. My fever began to subside and with the help of the aspirin the pain became tolerable. I still could not walk and my legs looked like two sticks. They were wrapped in heavy cotton to keep them warm. There was no heat in the apartment. The only warmth came from a cooking stove and wood or coal was hard to find. Food too was scarce and yet there was always some food for me. Benno never left my side. He slept on the floor next to me and when I was not sleeping he read to me. Often the only reading material available was the medical books in the office and he would sit and read. Just hearing his voice near me was calming.

We did not know where Pappi was and could not get word to Brzostek. Uncle Julek knew that we were in Tarnow, but where? The house he had brought us to was bombed and no one knew where we had gone. The Germans had invaded and there was a strict curfew. No one was allowed outdoors before sunrise or after sundown. It was winter and the days were very short. In the middle of one night someone knocked on the door. It was Pappi. He found us after spending nearly two weeks in Tarnow looking for us. He checked with all the hospitals and doctors and miraculously found the doctor who had given us shelter. She worked in a hospital and since we were all crowded into her apartment she spent most of her nights in the hospital.

Now my recovery began. Pappi was able to get food, wood for the stove and the all-important aspirins. In addition, seeing me alive he brought much cheer to us. He was full of jokes about the army and told us to be patient. We trusted him. Often I would wake in the morning to the soft sound of prayer. Papi and Benno standing near the window in their Tefillim and Talleisim (Phylacteries and Tallit) reciting the Shachrit (morning) prayers. Such a comforting sound. At one time during our stay in Tarnow Pappi went with Uncle Julek back to Katowitze to retrieve our winter clothing and much of our linens, blankets, carpets, dishes and paintings. We had one small painting that was an original. Before we left Berlin, Mutti took that painting off the wall and kept it with her throughout our precarious journey. If we lost everything, that small painting would help keep us from hunger for the rest of our lives. I do not remember who the artist was. It was a still life and it was beautifully framed.

Late December it was decided that we have to make our way to Brzostek. There was a strict curfew and no one was permitted to leave the city. One day Mutti got dressed in her best coat, hat and shoes and went out. She returned with two German officers who offered to help carry me into their car. She had encountered them in the street and told them that she was a Volksdeutsche (Germans living in Poland), that her husband was serving in the army and that she had a sick child who she wanted to bring to the estate of distant relatives in a nearby town. Pappi saw her approach from the window and retreated to another part of the apartment. I was wrapped up and carried into their car and we started out for Brzostek. What an enormous chance my mother took, how brave she was!

We arrived and she insisted that they deposit us at the post office and that she will send word to the estate to have someone come and pick us up. She spoke to the postmistress in Polish and told her to keep absolutely quiet until the officers leave. They were very reluctant to leave us but eventually they did. Mutti was petrified that someone would come to the post office, recognize her and start talking Yiddish to her. When the officers drove away she almost collapsed. As soon as the car drove off people who had watched through their windows came running and got a sled and transported me to Uncle Bergman's house, which was only about a quarter of a block away. Several nights later Pappi and Benno joined us, and for the moment we were a family united.

My grandmother, who was the healer, came with her various ointments and potions and administered daily massages to my useless legs. After about a month I was able to stand up and with much encouragement began to take some timid steps. Never were we closer than during that time. I began to gain strength and all the family rejoiced at my recovery. Mostly Pappi and Mutti and Benno. They had been told that I did not have a chance to survive and here I was free of fever, still some pain which was to last for a very long time, but visibly getting stronger every day.

When the Germans occupied Poland, Brzostek became home to part of the cavalry and their horses. The town became a ghetto to make room for the Germans. Jews from outlying areas were moved into town and homes that were once one family dwellings had to accommodate two or three families. Uncle Begman's house was divided in half. We were given the large kitchen and one bedroom. The front half of the house was occupied by three Polish adults: an elderly mother with her son and daughter. The son was an official at the town hall where he had an important position. They were very nice to us and he often was able to get us some extra wood for heating. Grandfather's house was already occupied by three families: Tante Reisel Meierowicz, with her husband and three children and the widow of my grandmother's brother (Benjamin) Tante Laya Schlanger with one of her daughters, Malka. They were living in Krakow and when the war started decided to leave and wait out the war in the little town. Tante Laya owned a little house on the same block as my grandparents, which was occupied by a widow. This widow was supposed to have moved in with her son and daughter but refused to vacate the little house. I believe she was mentally deranged. One time Tante Laya went to get some of her belongings from the attic and was attacked by this woman. She was severely beaten and eventually died of her wounds. Tante Laya was also the mother of Regina Miller and Avrum Schlanger. Malka went back to Krakow and later joined the partisans. She was high spirited and a rebel. I liked her a lot. She did not survive.

We stayed with Uncle Bergman. Our parents were determined to keep our minds active. Jewish children were not permitted to attend school nor were there any libraries. The youngest daughter of the local rabbi, Beila, had gone to seminary in Cracow and was a teacher at a girls school. At the beginning of the war she came home to Brzostek. Soon she became our teacher. We learned the Chumash, the Five Megillot and Pirkey Avod. All in Hebrew translated by Beila. Tuska was a part of our little group. I firmly believe that the lessons learned then played an important part in our development. They were the building blocks of our character and moral integrity. I know that these lessons have helped me later on through some hard times and decisions. Teaching was forbidden and had Beila been caught the consequences would have been imprisonment or worse. She carried a bag with knitting, embroidery and playing cards with her. Had she been caught she would make believe that she had just come for a social evening. She was very brave and dedicated. I loved her very much. She did not survive the war.

Sometime around Sukkot 1940, we received word that my grandfather Aaron had died. My father applied for a travel permit and was granted one but much too late for his father's funeral. He left for Ranirzow, stayed with his mother and sisters for 10 days and then on the way home stopped in Lodz. The intent was to get some warm clothing for Benno and me since we had outgrown what we had. Lodz was known for many tailoring establishments. When my father arrived home he was a changed man. He had witnessed the treatment of the Jews and early deportations from the Lodz Ghetto and realized that we had the same fate to look forward to. He hugged us and cried. It was then that he explained to us why his father never spoke to him. Grandfather wanted his oldest son to follow in his footsteps and become a Shochet. Our father rebelled against that and ran away from home at a very young age. Even though he eventually did very well in every respect, supported the little synagogue in Ranizow, built a Mikva (ritual pool) and helped care for all his siblings, Grandfather never fully forgave him. It hurt Pappi very much and he cried when he told us about it. Never hang on to grievances, forgive and if possible forget, that is what he often told us. Now we understood a lot more about his relationship with his mother and brothers. Pappi's hair had turned gray and he lost his appetite and couldn't sleep. We would hear him tossing and turning and often cry out when he finally fell into a restless sleep.

Sometime during that late fall, at about 4 o'clock in the morning we heard a knock on the window of our bedroom. A little voice calling, "Tante Gina, let me in, I am cold." It was little Renie. She had been playing in the house of a neighbor in Tarnow. When she came home before curfew, the house was boarded up. Tante Hella and Gunther had been deported. Destination unknown. Little Renie with the help of a friendly neighbor started out for Brzostek. They walked 45 kilometers in the dark and made their way to our house. Renie became my little sister and slept in the bed with me and my mother. Uncle Joseph's efforts to locate Tante Hella and Gunther were fruitless. Those were the earliest warning signs of what was in store for us. It was the beginning of a fear that haunted me and lasted throughout the war. The dread of a knock on the door any time of day or night became omnipresent. I became aware that people can just disappear without a trace. My parents began to look for a hiding place for us. Uncle Julek knew a farmer and this farmer agreed, for a large sum of money, to create a room in his barn for us. Pappi began to scrounge around for food supplies, blankets and some essential survival items. It was done in a very clandestine manner. Only the immediate family knew about it. I was not allowed to tell Tuska nor could we share the secret with our beloved teacher Beila.

The winter of 1940-1941 was extremely cold and some nights the water in the house froze. We were now none people living in a kitchen and one bedroom. Fetter Elle, his adopted daughter Gittel, her husband Menachem and their little boy all slept in the kitchen. Mutti, Renie and I shared the only bed in the bedroom. Pappi slept on a divan (couch) and Benno on the floor. In spite of the crowded quarters there were never any fights. Food was hard to get but the farmers who were trading never made so much money in their lives, and so we were never hungry. We all ate the same things, with the exception of the two-year-old boy for whom milk was made available before any of us would get it. In spite of the fear, which was in our conscious or unconscious, I have very warm memories of that time. Even our father, once he set a survival plan into motion, regained some of his humor.

At some point the horses, which had been housed in the synagogue, developed some sort of disease and many of them died. Of course, sabotage was suspected and the curfew became even more strict. Anyone seen outside before sunup or after sundown was shot at random. Benno, Renie and I invented games, read a lot and played with the little boy. The whole family played dominos or cards. My mother taught Renie and me a lot of songs and thus an atmosphere of some normalcy prevailed. When the weather got warmer and the earth thawed, my father with the help of Menachem and Benno began to dig in the woodshed in back of the house. A large crate was fabricated and all the silver candelabras and cutlery was wrapped in linen and towels and packed into the crate. An earthen jar, about the size that could hold one quart of liquid, was filled with gold dollar coins. This and the crate were lowered into the deep hole in the woodshed. We all had to memorize the exact location measured by the number of feet from the main house. My parents had paper dollar bills in large denominations. These were placed in-between the soles of our boots.

In 1950 I got a letter from Uncle Siegmund Salz, Tante Hellas' husband. He had survived in Siberia and came back to Poland with two women friends, looking for the remnants of his family. Through Uncle Solomon in Israel he got my address in New York and wrote to me asking for help to get out of Poland. At that time I believed that I would never go back to Poland and so after some deliberation, I gave him the information to find the buried treasures. He hired some people who agreed to dig for him with the arrangement that he share half of the find with them. Uncle Siegmund took a great chance. If they did not find the loot they would surely have killed him. Even if they did find it, he was not sure what they would do to him. In the end they did find the crate with silver and claimed that there was no sign of the earthen jar filled with gold coins. Who knows? In any case, the proceeds from this find got three people out of Poland and eventually to Israel.

Now comes the hard part, memories which still tear at my heartstrings. Seventy years have passed and the events are as clear in my mind's eye as if they happened last year. The pain of the memories is not as sharp as it used to be. That is why I can write about it.

Around Purim 1942 we were awakened at dawn by bullhorns and ordered out of our beds to assemble in the town square. We grabbed what we could to cover ourselves and went to the square. There we were separated into groups. Men and young boys in one line, women and children in another line, and old people to another side. The announcement came that young men were needed for work, would be well treated and would return home shortly. Without any time to consider what was happening. the young men and boys were herded onto trucks. My brother Benno was among them. I noticed that he did not have a warm jacket, only trousers over his pajamas and his boots. Without thinking of possible consequences I ran into the house, grabbed his jacket, stuffed some bread in it and flew over to the truck where he was with a large group of boys. I threw the jacket to him, he caught it and threw me a kiss with his hand. At that moment the SS man guarding the truck bent down and smashed my face with the butt of his rifle. I lost my balance from the impact, fell and hit my head on a large corner stone and passed out. When I regained consciousness my mother was holding me, I was bleeding from a broken nose and broken front teeth and a deep gash in the back of my head. I got up with the help of my mother and grandmother at the moment the trucks began to move out. Every time I hear and sing the Hatikva I still hear the sound of the trucks and the voices of those young men singing the Hatikva. I never saw my beloved brother Benjamin again. My mother told me that while I was unconscious my grandmother straightened my nose, which was squashed to one side, and applied pressure to stop the bleeding. I do remember the severe pain.

A short time later, on a balmy spring day, children were playing in front of their homes and in the square. Suddenly trucks came and over the bullhorn came the announcement that there is a very nice place for children where they will be properly cared for while their parents will go to work for the German army. With unbelievable speed the children were gathered and loaded onto the trucks. My little cousins Dvora and Lea, Tante Reisel's children, were among them. They were screaming for their mother and Tante Reisel came flying out of the house holding little Jeshiale in her arms. She offered to go with them, to help take care of all the children but to no avail. Little Jeshiale was screaming on the top of his lungs with his little arms tight around her neck. One of the German guards walked over and tried to take him from his mother. He screamed even louder and Tante Reisel tried to calm him down. We heard the commotion and came running. The Polish volunteer guards were standing by, keeping everyone at bay. At that moment the German guarding the truck grabbed a hold of Jeshiale and with inhuman force wrenched him from his mother's arms. He strode over to Grandfather's house and smashed the child's head against the stone wall until he was silenced. This was no accident of war, this was a deliberate killing of a child. What kind of person can do such a thing? How does one come to terms with such inhumanity? How does one ever look at another German without remembering this? Tante Reisel sat on the ground holding her dead child banging her head against the wall. The trucks moved away with wailing children never to be seen again. We buried little Jeshiale and the whole town came to sit with our family during the shiva period.

Some days later, it was market day in town and lots of people were milling around in the town square. Suddenly chairs and benches were being placed in the middle of the square. Then, with the help of Polish volunteers, Jewish men with beards and payot were rounded up and forced to sit on the benches and chairs. My grandfather Bezalel was one of them. My beautiful, proud, stately, highly respected grandmother, a true woman of valor, was brought in front of my grandfather holding a pair of big scissors which had been thrust into her hands. There she stood, looked at her husband, her mate with whom she brought 10 children into the world, married them off and they in turn had given her grandchildren and great grandchildren, and she shook her head. "No," she said. "Genig, enough, no more." And grandfather looked at her, shook his head, held her hands and repeated "Yo, genig, enough, no more." At that moment one of the Germans, alerted by a Polish volunteer, walked over and started poking grandmother in the ribs. Come, he yelled, you Jewish whore, get going. Our grandmother, our role model of dignity? I was about five feet away from them and saw grandfather's sad face. He kept repeating, "Genig, no more." The German was poking grandmother even harder and yelling at her.

At that moment, my beautiful grandmother turned to face him and spat in his face. There was a gasp all around. My mother held me tightly, I could hardly breathe and then, then I heard two shots. Both my grandparents were killed. Grandfather slumped in his chair and Grandmother fell to the side of him. People began to scream, Jews and Poles alike. People started running in every direction and then the shooting began. My mother let go of me and yelled "Ruth run, run and save yourself." And like the obedient child I was, though scared beyond reason, I ran. It was a stampede, people running all over. I ran in back of Grandfather's house, through the garden, down the hill, running blindly. Bullets flying all around me, people screaming and falling. I turned to look for my mother but did not see her. I just kept running. Suddenly I tripped and fell into a rain ditch by the side of the road. There was some water in the ditch. I hardly noticed it. Fear, totally paralyzing fear, took hold of me and holding my breath I passed out.

When I regained consciousness it was almost dark. I felt cold and scared and became aware of heavy weight on top of me. I tried to move and could not. Then I heard boots marching down the road. Slowly, ever so slowly they came closer. I heard moans and then shots ringing out and then silence. I held my breath, buried my face in the mud and mercifully passed out.

It was very dark when I awoke. All I noticed was the cold and the heavy weight on top of me. Slowly I began to claw at the earth to rid myself of the weight. I did not try to find out what it was that weighed me down, I just had to get out. The weight on top of me were bodies but I shut that thought out. After a long time I succeeded. I was shivering from cold and wet and did not know where to go. I sat and cried and very quietly began to call for my mother. No one answered. Suddenly, I remembered the instruction of my parents. Were we ever to be separated, we were to go to the Polish farm outside of town and wait. And so I made my way there. How I found them I cannot fathom even now. It was pitch black and the road was littered with corpses. I kept falling, got up again and again and by some miracle found the farmer's house. I knocked and they opened the door. I saw myself reflected in the horrified look of their faces. My face was full of mud, almost unrecognizable, and the rest of me was covered with blood. They immediately took me in, stripped my clothing, washed me and put me to bed. They burned my clothing and at dawn sent their young son to find my parents. I had fallen into a deep sleep, the sleep of youth. When I awoke the sun was streaming in through a window high up in the wall. I turned my head and saw my mother's head resting at the foot of the bed. For a moment I was afraid to stir. I remember thinking that I was dead and in heaven. And then memory returned and my mother awoke. She had brought clothing for me and after I dressed we ate some breakfast. My mother hugged and kissed the farmer's wife and then we returned to town. We did not know where my father was. The town was a town of mourning. All day long there were funerals. My grandparents were buried. It was Thursday, a few days before Pesach, April 1942. I was totally exhausted and remember almost nothing of the rest of the day.

The Germans came looking for my father. He was the only one in the town registered with a driver's license. Since he was not among the dead or the ones who had been sent to work camps, they wanted him now. My father had jumped into a cesspool in back of the house. At night he crawled out, walked to the river and bathed and then went to the farmer. They again sent word to my mother who came with clothing for him. I remember waking up finding my father at home. Where and how to hide him now? By midday the Germans took 10 hostages for my father. When he heard about that he went to the town hall and surrendered. Late afternoon we learned that my father would be sent away and that we could come to say goodbye to him. Tante Rondzia, a neighbor, my mother and myself walked to the town hall. My father came out with a German guard who ordered him to get onto a wagon waiting to take him away. My father began to negotiate with the German and after a few minutes my father walked over to where we were standing. He stopped in front of me, put his hands on my head and in a clear loud voice recited the traditional blessing of the Cohanim. He then bent down, kissed me and said quietly, only I, my mother and aunt heard him. "You my child shall live, you shall live to tell it all." He then hugged and kissed my mother and my aunt and left. Here I am seventy years later and I still can conjure up the feel of his hands on my head. I never fail to remember that moment when the blessings are recited in synagogue. There was a time when I could not listen to that; I wanted to run away, never to get back to temple to hear it. But, then you my children came along and when one does something for a child nothing is too difficult.

The very next day the man who shared the house with us informed us that there will be an "akzion" (known as round up) in town and he advised us to get away before it is too late. Fetter Elle, his daughter, her husband and the little boy decided to stay and "ride out" the storm. Mutti went to the farmer who had built a shelter for us but this time he was afraid to take us in. He told us that he heard there were people in the forest and we should go there. It was a great disappointment. He was afraid for his own life and the life of his family.

Mutti, little Renie and I put on several layers of clothing and our boots, which had dollars in between the soles, and late afternoon walked out of town. We hoped to be able to connect with these people who supposedly were forming groups in the woods. At that time the word "partisan" was not known to us. We walked until we reached the forest, found no one and when it got dark we sat down and rested. We had very little food with us since we could not carry anything that would arouse suspicion. We each had bread and fruit in our pockets. That would have to keep us fed until we could get some food from farmers. To this day, when I pass a dense forest, I remember that journey. It was pitch black in the forest and we had no blanket on which we could sit. The ground was damp and soon we were chilled to the bone. Renie and I fell asleep with our heads on Mutti's lap. She was propped up against a tree. When we awoke it was dawn and Mutti could not move her legs. All night she stayed still, not to disturb our much needed sleep, and circulation was cut off from both her legs. She was in great pain. We started to massage her and after what seemed a very long time (the sun was high already) she was able to get up. We ate our fruit and Mutti decided to find more food for us from some farmers. Renie and I stayed huddled in the forest and waited for her return. We were scared but neither of us admitted it. Mutti came back with just some rotten apples and no bread. The farmer whom she approached would not help her and told her that she can take the apples from the ground and get out fast. We continued to walk, found some berries and finished the rest of the bread we had brought from home. We crossed a brook and drank the water from it.

In the late afternoon we came to a clearing. There were cows grazing in a field and again Mutti went by herself to get some food. Renie and I stayed hidden. Renie cried and I remember holding her like a baby in my arms. I was so scared but did not want to show it. I was only 16 years old and at times I too wanted to cry. Suddenly we heard dogs barking. I shall never forget the sight of my mother running, being chased by dogs. The farmer refused to help her and sent the dogs after her. We retreated deeper into the forest; three "criminals" on the run. We walked endlessly and spent the nights hungry and cold in the forest. I have no idea how many days and nights we spent in the forest, time seemed endless. And then one day we came again to a clearing. We were on a hill and saw barracks in the valley. There was a fence around the area and as we were watching, a truck with people arrived and they entered a large gate. Another night in the forest and early in the morning we saw people come out of the gate, get onto waiting trucks and leave. Mutti decided that we might find some members of the family there and we should try to smuggle into the area if and when the people return in the evening. We shed our extra clothing, threw them and our boots into a ravine and made our way in the direction of the barracks. And indeed the trucks came back and we walked into (unbeknown to us) Camp Pustkow with the rest of the people.

People began to walk in the direction of their barracks and we followed. They seemed extremely tired and dirty. Mutti told us to look, maybe we can find Pappi and Benno. A siren sounded and people came out of their barracks and assembled making a large circle. We stood behind some people who began to ask us who we were and where we came from. Then suddenly I was grabbed by my arm and a voice whispered, "Go into this barrack and crawl under the beds and don't make a sound until I return." I did not recognize the voice or the face but Mutti seemed to know who it was and we disappeared into the barrack and crawled under what looked like planks of wood which we soon found out served as beds. It was dusty and smelly and we covered our mouths and noses to avoid sneezing. And we waited. After what seemed like a long time, people came and began climbing onto the planks. We did not know what they were doing. They were eating their meager daily rations of watery soup and bread. After some more time, that same voice announced, "Schwester und Brieder," sisters and brothers, we have souls among us who need saving. She then called my mother's name and told us to come out from under the "beds." It was my mother's cousin Mania Tugenthaft. Are there words in the English dictionary that can describe that scene? I don't think so. People looked at us and there was shock, pity, fear and indignation that we three could endanger all their lives. No one can possibly imagine OUR fear, our hunger and despair. Mutti held both of us and told them that we cannot go on and that we are at their mercy. Renie started to cry and so did I. There was some talk and the decision was made to hide us under the roof. We were hoisted up into an opening in the ceiling and crawled into a space under the tin roof. We could not sit up, not even get on our knees, we could barely turn from side to side. Then they handed a bucket up to us and everyone gave us little pieces of their bread. It was black bread mixed with saw dust and almost impossible to digest. We were told that we had to stay there until the "kappos" (designated Jewish overseers) made their final rounds of inspection. I know that I lost all sense of time. Renie and I kept falling asleep — the blessing of youth. Did we stay there all night that first night? I cannot tell. All I know is that the fear, the all-encompassing feeling that we are doomed never left me. During the day the sun was burning on the tin roof and at night it was bitter cold. I was afraid to ask Mutti what we will do next. Where are we? What is Camp Pustkow? Will we stay in that crawl space forever? Where is Benno and Pappi? Why are we hiding instead of going down and registering to work like all the other people? These were the thoughts that haunted me when I was awake. We heard the kappo come in, talk to the people for a few minutes and leave. Then Mania would come up and hand us some more food and drink and take away the little bucket with our waste. During the day, when everyone was at work we came down and moved around the barracks. As soon as the sun began to set we hid again. One night there was a lot of commotion. The boards were moved and another person crawled up to our space. It was a young woman whose experiences were similar to ours. Mutti talked with her in whispers and we found out that the camp was near Dembica, that people from all surrounding villages were brought here and all those who were able to work were being taken to a nearby ammunition repair factory. How long did we stay up there? I have no idea. I got sick with severe diarrhea and excruciating stomach pain. From that point on, Mania would take me down every night after the inspection and would keep me in bed with her. There is a memory that haunts me. It was in the middle of the night, loud voices were heard from outside and then crying. After a brief moment shots rang out and heart-wrenching screams followed. Bone-chilling screams. Mania covered my ears but I heard it anyway. And then, quite unexpectedly the kappo appeared. He was going to inspect the barracks to see if anyone was missing or if any illegal occupants were hiding. There was some rumor in camp about such "illegals." Mania pushed me under her blanket, in between her legs and, never lost for words, began to scream at the kappo. "We work all day, at least let us sleep at night." She yelled and all the other people followed suit. The kappo looked and then turned around and left. From that moment on we stayed hidden and only came down from our hiding place when no one was around. Days turned into weeks. Time was lost to me. I remember one morning a lot of people were whistling. It could be heard throughout the camp. Mutti said that it must be Yom Kipur and since no one had a shofar, they whistled the sounds of Tekia to let people know what day it is.

At some point in time I got sick with dysentery. Mania had been in contact with Uncle Josef who was in another section of the camp. The decision was made between them that I would have to leave camp with false papers and somehow make my way to Dembica. Uncle Josef told Mania that Tuska and her mother were hidden someplace and that the two of us should go together and try to get to Germany as Polish slave laborers. Suddenly there was talk of a false birth certificate to be made for me. Since the initials of my name were RW, I wanted my new name to have the same initials so that I could keep my cherished signet ring, which my father had given me for my birthday. I became Wanda Rasinska. Tuska who was Tuska Schmidt, became Teresa Kowalska. I was excited about the prospect of leaving the camp, never realizing that I would go without my mother and little Renie. It was the day before I was to go and Mutti was telling me not to eat and not to speak. To let Tuska do all the talking. My German accent was noticeable and could prove to be dangerous. Aren't you coming with me, I asked? No, no, I will follow later. Better go alone and then we will meet, she said. It is now seventy years later and I still cannot write about it without incredible pain. How could she do that to me? That is all I could think of at the time. I cried practically all night and after a long time fell asleep curled into Mutti. I don't remember waking and walking with all the people to the gate.

That was the last time I saw my mother. She was standing about six feet away from me, clutching the hand of my little cousin. She had pushed me just moments before, pushed me away from her, tears streaming down her face. There she stood so tall, so sure that she was doing the right thing and I, hating/loving her the way only a child can hate a parent. She seemed so strong, so sure that she was doing the only thing that made sense at that chaotic time. Her last words of promise to follow soon, I knew even then were not to be true. Don't speak, she admonished again. I had been in Poland only five years, only two years in school, speaking only German at home. My accent would surely give me away. That push into the hands of Tuska who pulled me with her was certainly more painful than giving birth. But, I, I did not know or want to know. How I hated her at that moment. Her and little Renie, innocent little Renie. Why is she holding her, she is MY mother, she should be holding ME. There she stood holding her instead of me. I, who was so scared, sick with dysentery, the common disease in camp, was being pushed into the unknown. She looked so tall my mother, my Mutti, so determined in spite of the tears, so all knowing, nodding her head. And then she turned and left and I had no place to go but follow Tuska. I was outside the gate and could not turn back. To this day, I do not remember the next few days. Now, in the autumn of my life, how I wish that I had had the chance to say "I am sorry darling Mutti, I did not understand what you did for me. I love you more than you will ever know for your strength, for giving me life twice."

I have tried numerous times to recall the events that followed. They must have been so deeply traumatic that I shut out all memory. I know only what Tuska tells me. We had a guide who was a friend of Tuska's stepbrother Reuven Goldman. He took us to the train station where Polish farm workers were being transported to Krakow and then on to Germany. He told me to take off my ring since Polish farm workers did not wear any rings. I did and put it in my mouth and forced it around a tooth. That part I do remember. It was rather painful, did not fit initially, but I kept biting down and pushing and eventually the tooth moved and the ring fit around it. Years later a dentist in Neckargemund cut the ring off and I lost the tooth to decay. The guide also told us to look cheerful and keep our heads high and mingle with the other people. What I remember from that journey to Krakow was the pain and continuous diarrhea. I was frightened and wanted to cry but had to pretend to be happy like the rest of the Polish girls who looked forward to the adventure of travel. Most of them had never left their homes and villages and this was a chance to see the world. Once, when most people left the train to get some food and water that was being distributed on the platforms, I stayed curled up in a fetal position with terrible burning pain. I had not bathed, showered or washed and my anus was inflamed and hurt all the time. There was a German traveling with us as a guard or overseer. One of his hands had a wooden prosthesis. He came over to me where I was laying curled up, touched my shoulder and handed me a bar of Suchard chocolate. He spoke German and of course I understood but had to pretend that I did not know what he was talking about. He then motioned for me to eat it quickly before any one comes back. I did, and soon began to feel better. The combination of the cocoa (which is binding) and the sugar and milk gave me a tremendous boost. That little act of kindness in the midst of the chaos I left behind restored some of my hope that maybe all humanity was not lost. By the time we reached Krakow my diarrhea was somewhat controlled and I was able to eat some of the food.

The events that followed are blurred. I remember giving away all my clothing for delousing and getting a chance to wash. It was only then that the burning in my anus abated. We were given straw sacks and pillows and an army blanket to cover up with. Tuska and I were in separate corners of the large gymnasium. We had to make sure that if one of us is discovered the other one would be safe. I was terribly afraid and in the middle of the night I coughed quietly. After a few moments there was a cough from the other corner of the room. There was Tuska, my life line, my anchor. I know that I would never have come that far were it not for her strength and support.

The next morning we were told to fluff our pillows and mattresses (straw pallets). We still did not have our clothing and covered ourselves as best as we could with the blanket. I was bent over doing my chore when I heard boots approaching. They were coming closer and closer and I froze in my bent-over position with just the blanket to cover my nudity. Suddenly I was whipped across my backside and I let out a gasp and straightened to face a German guard. He was in uniform, blond with a mustache and a vicious grin on his face. He put the whip under my chin, lifted my face and said (in German), "But you, you little one, you understand what I am saying." I looked at him without blinking an eye, completely dumb-founded. Others stood around me and watched as he turned with a curse, "You Polish pig," and left.

I have little or no recollection of what happened from that point on until I reached Kummelbacher Hof in Neckargemund, Germany. This lack of memory attests the severity of my trauma.

Tuska was sent to a smaller farm owned by a couple and I was at Kummelbacherhof, which was owned by I.G. Farben and served as a rest home for their employees. I.G. Farben was the chemical company that produced the cyclone gas used in the gas chambers of the concentration camps. The farm was self-sustaining, supervised by some order of Sisters of, I believe, the Lutheran church. The head Sister's name was Schwester Hanna. When she looked me over she shook her head in dismay. Children they send us to work, she said. What am I supposed to do with this one? She took me over to Freulein Emilie, the cook in charge of the large kitchen, and told her to put me to work. I was then assigned to a room with another Polish girl who had been there for some time. Her name was Helena and she was severely cross-eyed. I was afraid to speak (I believed that I had a strong accent even though Tuska assured me that I did not) heeding my mother's last words. Helena watched me and would wake me early in the morning, before we even had to get up, to make sure that we say our prayers together. I knew no prayers in Polish so not speaking was certainly to my benefit. Out of the corner of my eye I watched whenever she crossed herself and moments later I would follow suit. I crossed myself and prayed. I said the Sh'ma and the morning prayer, which I knew by heart. "Thou shall love thy God with all thy heart and all thy soul." I used to say these prayers at home since I was a little girl and now when I read them in temple I have that vision of that young girl kneeling, crossing herself and praying with all her heart and soul. I never knew if Helena was watching me or not because of her eye condition. I was terribly afraid of her and afraid that I might speak in my sleep and she would hear me and find out that I am Jewish. I would wait until I heard her deep breathing before I allowed myself some sleep. The chances were that if she knew she would report me and I would be arrested or worse, sent back.

By now it was late fall and most workers were assigned to harvesting in the fields. I was put in back of the kitchen with a huge bag of potatoes, a large pail filled with water. I was told to peel the potatoes and then put them into the water. I had never in my life peeled potatoes and things were not going well for me. Freulein Emilie would come out several times and show me what to do. She was not pleased with me and kept shaking her head in disapproval. I was outside and heard the birds and the call of a cuckoo. To me it sounded as if my mother was calling "Ruuuth". I started to cry and could not stop. I was sobbing and it seemed that I was washing the potatoes with my tears. Freulein Emilie called Schwester Hanna who came out to see for herself what was happening. She spoke softly to me (in German) "Child why are you crying, are you in pain?" The kinder she spoke the more I cried. Freulein Emilie came over with some cookies and all I did is shake my head and cry. Finally, Schwester Hanna said to the cook that she would call the workers bureau and have them send me home. When I overheard that, I stopped crying. Luckily it was a weekend and the office was closed. I never cried again at work and made an effort to improve with my assigned work. As arranged with my mother, I sent a postcard to the woman who had shared the house with us in Brzostek to tell her where I am and that all is very good for me. Through Mania and Uncle Josef this contact was established and I know that my mother got the news. I have a letter (sent to me by that woman) that my mother wrote to her from Pustkow asking her to send me some winter clothing. This letter is the only thing I ever got from her.

Most of the time I scrubbed huge pots, peeled potatoes, carrots and sometimes apples. Was I hungry? There was a gnawing pain in the pit of my stomach. It was not physical hunger, it was emotional hunger, a void that could not be sated with food. Afraid? Yes! All the time! Now, even more afraid of my Polish co-workers than the Germans. They called me the "dummy" and would take the best pieces of food first and leave scraps for me. We ate in a separate room near the kitchen away from the German workers and permanent staff.

After two weeks I had time off on a Sunday afternoon. Somehow (I don't remember how) I found out that Tuska was working on a farm not far from Neckargemund. We established contact and met Sunday afternoon in the little village and sat on a bench and compared our lives. I had a pair of sandals and exchanged these for Tuska's wooden clogs until the next time we would meet. When we parted I was miserable and cried all the way back to the farm. I was still scared of my co-workers. I was homesick and needed the comfort of having Tuska with me. It took close to six months before we were reunited. The small farm she had been placed on did not need her during the winter months and so she asked to be sent to work at Kummerlbacher Hof. She was the brave and strong one.

My memory of that early time is filled with fear. I did not allow myself to face the situation I was in. Don't think, just keep going from one day to the next. Pappi said I would live, and so I have to make sure that I go on until we meet again. Don't think, don't think, just keep moving and do your work. I had bad dreams and often awakened screaming. Helena, my roommate, became very suspicious and I heard her tell the other girls. There was one big girl, named Bronka who felt sorry for me. She told Helena to stop bothering me and leave me be. She is a dummy and does her work, so leave her alone, she would tell her whenever Helena started to pick on me.

Once Tuska came to Kummelbacherhof my life improved drastically. Tuska said that we were from the same town and asked to share the room with me. So, we were moved together into a room which was not in the main house. From that time on I was less afraid and life became more orderly in a regimented way. We worked ten, sometimes twelve to fourteen hours a day but we were together at night. Tuska would wake me up if I screamed and made me talk. She was afraid that I had suffered a severe shock and actually lost my speech. After some time I began to sleep more peacefully and began to talk. No one paid much attention to me or to the change. In the autumn there was different kind of work. After the field harvest there was the harvest from the orchards. Pigs were slaughtered, canning began and closer to the Christmas holiday preparations were made for guests who would be arriving for the Christmas week. Daily chores included milking cows, cleaning the stalls, preparing the guest rooms, laundry and kitchen clean up. I was assigned to the chicken farm. In addition to collecting eggs, the chicken coops needed to be scraped and cleaned daily. There were four sheep which I was taught to milk and after I learned, I liked that the best. They were warm and furry and I used to love to warm my hands and sometimes feet in their pelt. There was a dog which came sometime during my early stay. She was a German shepherd puppy and from the day she got there I was in charge of feeding her. She was a loving puppy and became attached to me. As soon as I came up the hill in the morning I would let her out of the pen and she would follow me all over the place. Her name was Bella. Schwester Doerthe was in charge of that part of the farm and I was responsible to her. Sometimes she would scold me for something I did not do correctly and then Bella would bare her teeth and growl at her. Bella became a very good watchdog and my good friend. In the chicken house there was a mechanical incubator for the eggs, which were fertilized. I learned how to check the eggs under a light and place them in the incubator. The temperature and humidity had to be watched every two hours until the chicks hatched. I liked this part of my work. There is life on a farm in many forms. Chicks hatch, cows and sheep have calves and lambs, and the cycle of life is constant. There was also food. Many times when I fed the pigs I would snatch some of their food like potatoes or corn. Working outdoors produced quite an appetite and it seemed that there never was enough food to satisfy. But, as long as I did not think about my immediate past I was fine. The stench of decay and death stayed with me since Pustkow. I thought that I would never be able to get rid of it. But I had youth in my favor and I began to gain weight and every now and then I caught myself laughing with Bella frolicking at my side. And I had that direct link to the past, a link to normalcy. Tuska was with me.

Once I was called to help in the main house. An inspection from I.G. Farben was coming and the house and offices had to be scrubbed from top to bottom. I was told to clean Schwester Hanna's office. When I came in with my cleaning utensils I noticed that instead of the picture of Hitler, which I had seen on the wall in back of her desk when I first arrived, there was the picture of the Kaiser. She noticed my surprise and said "Ach, I forgot all about this." She quickly took the picture off the wall and replaced it with the one of Hitler and then motioned to me to keep quiet. Was she testing me? I don't know but at that moment there was an unspoken bond which I felt for her. Underneath her stern exterior there was a person with thought and feeling. She would often call me, sometimes on particularly bad weather days, to come and do "Ecken wishen," wipe the corners in her office.

During the Christmas holidays the house was full of guests. These were officials of I.G. Farben with their families and related soldiers who were home for the holidays. Some of us were needed to help in the kitchen and to serve at dinner time. There were two passages to and from the main dining room. We usually delivered the full trays to the waitresses and then took empty dishes away. Once I carried a full tray of fresh strawberries (from the hot house) topped with whipped cream. Of course none of that was ever available for us. My mouth watered and when I looked around Tuska was in back of me. I smiled at her and without a moments hesitation we spat into every one of the little dishes before we handed them over. Then we lingered a moment and with great relish watched the guests consume our spit with their dessert. That was almost better then eating it ourselves. Our private revenge.

These were special assignments. My daily chores had to be done. If any of us were needed in the kitchen or in the main house, it was just additional work.

One time I was working in the kitchen helping with cleanup. I stood on a step at the huge stove and was told to remove a large pot with potatoes. What I did not know or see was that the potatoes had been cooked in a double boiler. The pot with the boiling water had been removed moments before, placed on the floor, and when I stepped down from the upper step next to the oven holding the large pot in front of me, I stepped into the boiling water. I shall never forget the pain. When they removed the sock I was wearing, skin and flesh came off with it, exposing bone. I was taken to my room with just some butter on the wound and left there. I howled for hours until I lost my voice and probably passed out.

The next thing I remember there was a doctor looking at my leg, putting on salve and bandages and giving me something to drink and pills for the pain. He spoke very harshly to Schwester Hanna who was with him. It was hours after the accident and he could not understand why no one had called a doctor before. Even these slave workers are human beings, he said. Schwester Hanna was apologetic and explained that she had not heard of the accident until she was out walking near the little house where she heard me moaning. I often wondered if she realized that I understood what they were saying. The kitchen staff had kept it a secret. It was a long time until I recovered.

In early February 1943 I received a postcard. It was Uncle Josef's handwriting but without his signature. He wrote that my mother and little Renie went on a long holiday during Christmas and may not return. I should not expect any mail from them. It was a coded message telling me that they were sent away. Years later, in 1981 I inquired at Yad Vashem about Pustkow. It was then that I learned that on Chanukah 1942 Pustkow was liquidated. All ablebodied workers were sent to another camp but most women with children were shot and thrown into a mass grave. That is most likely what happened to my Mutti and little Renie.

During one of the holidays and visits of officials I was given a tray with food to deliver to the wife of a high official who had a cold and did not come to the dining room. I went to her room and when I set the tray down she reached into her bag and proceeded to give me a tip. I was stunned and shaken. Suddenly, this kind act reminded me of my present position. A total reversal of roles. How many times had I seen my mother give tips to workers? I burst out crying and ran out of the room. The woman had no idea what happened and spoke about it to Schwester Hanna. She in turn called me into her office and asked why I ran away without taking the tip. I could not answer her, still making believe that I did not understand and just stood there gazing at her. She walked over to me and said, "Wanda, Wanda, who are you?" I looked into her eyes, shrugged my shoulders and left.

Later, in 1946, before we were to leave for the USA, Tuska and I went back to see her, to tell her all about us and let her know that we were leaving for America. She reminded me of that incident and said that she suspected all along that I was not one of the Polish workers. She then took off a little black locket in the shape of a heart from her neck and gave it to me. She told me, "It belonged to my grandmother, I have no children to pass it on to, so should you ever find pictures of your parents, put them in this locket." She also reminded me of an incident that took place in her office. "I don't know the date," she said, "but one day a young woman came to the office and asked to interview all the Polish workers. She was authorized to take a census of the workers and see if they needed help to establish contact with their families back home." One by one we came to the office. When my turn came Schwester Hanna saw enormous fear in my eyes. I had destroyed my identification papers (false birth certificate) after Marusia was deported. Now I had nothing to show this census taker. At one point the young woman asked very politely if she might have a cup of hot tea. Schwester Hanna left and momentarily the young woman pressed a tiny mezuza in my hand and whispered, "You are not alone, do not worry." When Schwester Hanna came back with the tea, the young woman said that she was done with me and I was dismissed. Schwester Hanna told me that her suspicion about me was confirmed and she knew that some day I would come and tell her everything.

You, my children, you all know that little locket which I wear all the time and that is the history of it.

There was a man in charge of the cow stalls, the milking and feeding and cleaning up. His name was Jupp Schaefer. Tuska worked with him. He was strange looking, very effeminate, prancing and dancing around during his work. Little by little Tuska found out that he was gay and had been in a concentration camp because of that. He was freed since there was an acute shortage of farm workers. He was on house arrest and had to remain at Kummelbacher Hof without any leave. He also had a radio and whenever possible he would tune in to the Polish news broadcast from England (which was of course forbidden) and then call Tuska to listen to the news. Thus we were aware of losses the German army took on the front with Russia. We were also the first ones to know about the American invasion at Normandy and our hopes skyrocketed. Soon, soon it'll all be over and we will go home to our parents. Deep down inside we knew that nothing would ever be the same, but we would not admit it to ourselves. We needed to hold on to hope.

There are some other memories but I am not sure which time slot they fit into. There was this lovely girl from the Ukraine. Her name was Marusia. I was once working next to her in the potato field. She used to hum or whistle all the time. Once I heard her whistle the tune to Hatikva. I allowed myself a look and she winked at me. Much later, Marusia did not appear at breakfast in the morning. We were told that she will not be back, that she was an enemy of the fatherland and was sent back home. We never heard about her again and Tuska and

I became even more cautious. She obviously was Jewish and became careless. Who recognized her and who turned her in? What would happen to us if she was tortured and gave my name? In my fear I tore up my false papers and swallowed them. We never found out what happened to her. I always suspected Helena. I never trusted her and avoided contact with her whenever possible.

At some point in time we met Rose who was working in Neckargemund and whose name was Katia. Tuska has more accurate memories of that time. Of course once liberated we stayed together and became friends. Her name was Rose Einsiedler and she lived in Los Angeles, California. She never fully recovered from the horrors she experienced. She was paranoid and used to keep a knife under her pillow. She is no longer alive.

Spring 1944 was lovely. Crocuses and forsythia bloomed and after rain there was a fresh smell all around. Birds were singing and the earth was full of renewal. One Tuesday afternoon Schwester Doerthe came to the chicken house and told me to go to Neckargemund (neighboring town) and pick up her precious antique clock from the watchmaker, which she had left there for repair. I left in good spirits because I loved the walk to the little town. I picked up the clock and started slowly to walk back up the hill to the farm. Three soldiers were on the road and they began to follow me. They were loud and boisterous. I got frightened and started to walk faster. They were now calling me and I started to run. Soon they ran after me and overtook me. When I did not answer them they realized that I was not German. Let's have some fun with this one, she looks clean, they said. They started pulling my hair and my clothing and I noticed that they smelled of beer. They were three and I was one. No matter how hard I tried to fight them off, I could not. They held me down and ripped my clothing. I cried and fought and the more I resisted the more they whooped. One of them took of his pants and stood over me with a huge erection. I started to scream, one of them held my hands, threw me to the ground. I spat, got slapped in the face and was gang raped.

When I was a little girl I had two constant companions. My brother Benno, my playmate, my protector and my role model. And I had GOD. The omnipresent God. The God I could pray to, the God I believed in as only a child can, with all my heart and soul. He was the God who always listened. When Benno was hit by a trolley car I prayed very hard and God listened and sent Benno home from the hospital with only minor bruises and a mild concussion. I never left his bedside. When Pappi was away on his business trips and we went to temple without him, I always prayed for his speedy return. And he always came home. I was convinced God had a hand in all that. We were always told that God listens to children first and foremost. It seemed that he always listened to me. Later, when Pappi was sent to Dachau, I prayed real hard and put my full trust in God. It took a while, but Pappi did come home. My faith was reinforced with all these positive experiences.

How was I to know that God, my God, my friend, would soon take a sabbatical? Through the darkest moments in my life my faith was with me like a cloak. In Pustkow the borders of that cloak of faith began to fray. The borders were not quite intact but I continued to pray. I needed God, I needed that anchor even later on when I was kneeling and praying, silently repeating the Shema and the morning or evening prayer.

That spring afternoon my God left me forever. He left me on the damp ground bathed in my own blood humiliated and raped. "Min Hametzar Carati Ya." Out of the depth I cried to Him, HE DID NOT HEAR ME, He stopped listening!

With my hands and fingers I scraped and dug a hole in the soft ground, buried my face and howled. When I had no voice left I buried God. The GOD of my childhood was gone, that God of the innocent child would never return. Martin Buber once asked his students if they could name one day or time when one would not acknowledge God. I would have told him the day and time when God did not see the young girl and she lost Him.

It was nearly dark when Schwester Doerthe came looking for me. She found me staggering on the road and soon realized what had happened to me. Her precious clock was smashed to pieces but she never scolded me. She took me to her private bathroom, put me in a tub of warm water and called Schwester Hanna. Their kindness made me cry even more. I needed my mother, my Mutti, I needed Benjamin, my Benno my protector. I needed to be held and comforted but not by Germans, not by them. In my mind they were kin to the enemy. I had lost everyone and everything, even my body, my sacred body was violated. It took many years to heal this wound. It is only now, in the autumn of my life that I can write or talk about this.

I continued to work. Farm life never stops, it does not care about people's feelings. And so I too went on. Numb with an internal pain, which cannot be put into words. Even now, as I write about it, I cannot allow myself to become emotional. I was a hurt child then and that hurt child is still in me. I have never fully outgrown the hurt. It haunts me often but when things get tough I take inventory. What I have now is more than I ever hoped for then and it does fill the deep void. I have often said that you, my husband and my beloved children, have done more to save my sanity then any therapy I might have had.

1944–1945 winter was particularly harsh. Every few nights we heard news about the fighting on the Eastern Front as well as the allied invasion. Jupp Schaefer would call us in the middle of the night and we went to his room above the cow shed and listened to the Polish radio station from England. We knew the end of the war was near. Early spring 1945 there were daily as well as nightly air raids. We, the Polish girls, did not go to the shelter. We stayed huddled in the kitchen and were full of cheer when we heard the heavy sound of the bombers overhead. One night we were in the kitchen corridor. Big Bronka looked at the big stove and pointed out the large buckets filled with milk kept there for the morning when the cream was skimmed off the top for butter. One of us stood watch for anyone coming from the shelter and the rest went to the buckets and scooped the cream off and gorged on it. We usually had enough food but never any fat and we were starving for it. When we were done we realized that now the buckets were not full. Again, it was Bronka who decided to just add water to fill them up. When the "all clear" sounded we left the kitchen. In the morning there was much head shaking and talk in the kitchen about the quality of the milk. The head cook decided that the cows are frightened by the air raids and that affects the fat contents of their milk. We were delighted.

It was time to prepare the fields for planting. One morning, when we got to the field, there was a cover of white leaflets that had been dropped by the British Air Force during the night. They warned people not to go to the fields. Planes could come any time and anyone found in the field would be shot. There were many scarecrows in the field. At first no one went but after some time we were told that we have to plant and to be careful. If we heard planes we were to throw ourselves on the ground until they past. One afternoon I was sent to the nearby field to get some new potatoes for the evening meal. Bella (the dog) was with me running around freely. Suddenly I heard the planes even before they came over the mountain. I called for Bella and she thought that I wanted to play with her. I ran to her and at that moment the firing started on the other side of the hill. I threw myself on the ground and Bella fell on top of me. She was scared, whined and licked my neck and ears. The planes came closer and within seconds bullets fell all around us. Bella shivered but did not move, just whined and whimpered. The whole incident took no more than a few seconds. When the planes left I waited a few minutes and then told Bella to get up. When she continued to whimper and not move I realized that she had been hit. I started to scream, picked her up and carried her down towards the house. The gardener came running towards me and helped me with Bella. I was hysterical and bloodied but not hurt. How many times could I escape injury or death? First it was Benno who covered me with his body to protect me from the chandelier crashing down on us and then this dog, a German dog. Had it not been for her I would have gotten the bullet. Bella had surgery to remove the bullet from her hip and although she recovered she was never able to run and play as before.

Now it was the beginning of the end. The town of Heidelberg, which is about 8 km. from Neckargemund, was never hit. It is a university town and many Americans had studied there. The town was spared but all bridges across the river Neckar were destroyed. Soon we saw German tanks moving and word came that they were fleeing from the Americans. Jupp Schaefer never failed to provide us with news. One night there was a hit and we lost all electricity. The chicks in the incubator were due to hatch in a few days. Without the correct temperature and humidity they would die. I stayed in the chicken house all day and at night by candlelight kept water boiling on the coal stove and watched the gauges. I had no food for the night. Tuska came with supplies that she had saved from dinner and I managed to stay awake. The thought of those little chicks dying bothered me terribly. They were so innocent. I looked upon them as children and myself as their rescuer. Schwester Doerthe relieved me during the day, I did my other chores and managed to sleep a few hours. My night vigil continued for three nights. All the chicks hatched and I was sure that I had saved their lives.

Now there was a lot of truck and tank movement on the main road. Then the shelling began. One morning, we were in the kitchen when suddenly there was a direct hit. All the windows shattered and people started running for shelter. We were told to run to the potato cellar which was in an adjacent building and to hide there. The staff from the main house all went to their shelter. Anna, one of the Polish girls panicked and threw herself on the floor screamed hysterically and would not move. I was near her and started pulling her by the legs out of the kitchen. It all happened so fast. I could not move her myself and decided to run for help. In moments big Bronka came, lifted Anna and carried her all the way to the cellar. She was very strong and somehow always there when needed. We, the Polish girls, and one of the German workers who was in charge of the barn, huddled in the cellar from where we could hear the firing upstairs. Then we heard footsteps and realized someone was coming down the stairs to where we were hidden. We hid behind potato sacks and held our breath. There was no electricity and it was completely dark. Two soldiers walked in with flashlights, they looked around holding their rifles with bayonets drawn. The German stood up with his hands over his head but before he had a chance to say anything they shot him. The sound of the shot in the dark cellar reverberated and awakened in me memory of past shooting. I started to scream NO! NO! They looked at us and motioned that we are free, that we can get out and then they turned and left. They must have thought that we were held prisoner and that the German was guarding us.

When I was a child in school in Germany we had learned some English. I learned children's poems like "Humpty Dumpty," "Little Miss Muffett" and "Peter Peter Pumpkin Eater," and some basic words. The NO! I screamed was an instinctive reaction to the shooting. I knew it was wrong of them to shoot this man, but I could not explain who he or we were. Some moments later Tuska and I ran to the main house and told Schwester Hanna what happened. The man was only shot in the arm and recovered.

The next hours and days are a blur. I don't know exactly when, but at some point I was sleeping and I must have had a nightmare. I started to scream and could not stop. Tuska was frantic. She ran to Schwester Hanna who came and sat with me. I have some vague memory of it. She looked sad, she listened to my screaming and kept shaking her head. Tuska told me that I screamed in Polish, German and even Hebrew. After what seemed like a long time, I was given a sedative and fell into a deep sleep.

The fighting subsided. There was a lot of movement of American tanks, trucks and jeeps on the main road. One morning a jeep came to the front of the main house. All workers were told to assemble. We stood in a line and of course, Tuska and I stood next to each other. There were four soldiers in the jeep. The driver, and two officers and one other soldier. One of the officers had a Star of David on his lapels and his cap. When I saw it my eyes almost popped out of my head. I was sure that there was a Jewish Army. Tuska and I held on to each other squeezing hands. The soldier who followed close behind the officers saw my face. As he walked by us he said in Yiddish, "Don't talk, we'll be back." Before they left they told us that we are free to leave. Free to leave? Where to? To whom? Home? Where is home?

We were intoxicated with the word. FREEDOM! The next morning at breakfast, we and the other Polish girls decided we would leave and go to Heidelberg. We gathered our meager belongings and left. We had no money, very few items of clothing and no place to go. But we left in high spirits and walked to Heidelberg. When we got there we had no place to stay and no food. We walked around for hours and finally found an empty railroad car on the outskirts of town and settled in. The following morning two American soldiers on patrol found us. When they realized that we were not Germans they told us to wait there until the American Red Cross comes who would then find us shelter. They were Jewish and one of them knew a little Yiddish, enough to communicate. They came back several times and brought us some food. One day they asked us if we need clothing and of course we said yes. They asked us to come with them and Tuska, Rose (who had come with us) and I went with them. The other girls warned us not to go. "They are soldiers, how can you trust them?" But we knew better.

We came to town and walked into an apartment house. They rang the bell of the first apartment and a woman opened the door. When she saw the soldiers with bayonets drawn she started screaming, picked up her hands and yelled, "I was not a Nazi," over and over again. Then

Phillip Stuchen, Leo Popowski and Ruth Wachner (Heidelberg, 1945)

Ruth Wachner and Tuska Schmidt (Heidelberg, 1945)

she moved away from the door to let us in. The soldiers motioned to us to go in and take what we need. We just stood there and did not move. Go, they said, she is German, go take what you need. The three of us looked at each other, shook our heads, turned around and left. One of the soldiers who spoke some Yiddish ran after us and asked if we are afraid. No, we told him, but if we do this, we are no better than they were. The soldier shook his head in disbelief and told us that he had gone to Hebrew school, he was a Bar Mitzva but forgot a lot. Yet the lesson he learned from us will stay with him forever. We met him later on again, his last name was Bialik and he was from Philadelphia.

Within several days we connected with the American Red Cross. We were given uniforms to supplement our own clothing and were assigned to a nearby schoolhouse for shelter. We were given forms to list the names of our families with the hope of finding someone. There were a lot of people, mostly Polish farm workers. In the school we shared a classroom with about 15 people. There were mattresses on the floor and army blankets. The American Red Cross had taken over the large public library in the middle of Heidelberg as a club for their soldiers. There was an endless supply of coffee and doughnuts. Some of us were assigned to serve the coffee and doughnuts and we were given blouses and skirts and little aprons that made us look like waitresses. At first we could not get our fill of doughnuts, which was an unknown pastry for us. This lasted about a week or so. Tuska and I spoke to the woman in charge and told her that we would like to work but not as waitresses. Soon I was assigned to a room in the library that was equipped with American magazines and paperback books. I met a lot of soldiers who used to come there to read and would stop and talk to me. Some spoke German and some of the Jewish boys spoke a little Yiddish. One day the soldier who had first seen us on the farm came in and was very happy to see me. After I told him a little about my past he came by every day and we became good friends. His name is David Tanzman and he lives in Detroit. We met Ruth and Margot Hollander who had survived with their mother and were living in Heidelberg. Their mother became a surrogate mother to us. She took us in, sheltered us when we needed comfort and was always there with a hug, food and advice. Tuska and I found a room that we rented from a German family. We had no money but they were happy to have us in exchange for some coffee and canned food, which we were able to get from the American soldiers who got it from the PX. David Tanzman and Chaplain Dicker organized a makeshift synagogue in a fraternity house adjacent to the university. Soon we were going to services on Friday evenings followed by an Oneg Shabat, which we, the Jewish girls, hosted. There was canned gefilte fish as well as challah baked by the army cook in the fraternity house kitchen. I cannot describe the atmosphere. For the soldiers it was a touch of home. For us it was a reminder of what we lost. David Tanzman told the soldiers to treat us as sisters, if they wanted other entertainment they would have to look elsewhere. And they did treat us royally. In the meantime, the American Red Cross instituted a search for our relatives. Tuska was by then working at UNRA (United Nations Relief Administration) and I had gotten a job with American Joint Distribution Committee (AJDC). My boss was a Canadian by the name of Phillip Stuchen. We became good friends. My job was mostly to interview people who came looking for relatives and to help them fill out forms. Since I spoke some Yiddish, German and Polish I was able to take down all the information and follow up with a search. I also met Leo Popowski who worked with me at AJDC and we became good friends. Both Tuska and I did get some pocket money although it was rather worthless since there was nothing in the stores that we could buy.

In the late fall of 1945 I got sick with the grippe (flu). I was running a high fever and stayed in bed. Tuska would come home at midday to make sure I had something to drink. One day, I had a very high fever and Tuska did not go to work. She stayed with me and kept applying cold compresses to bring down the fever. A young man came to the door. He asked for me but the landlady told him that I was sick and could not see anyone. He insisted that he had an important message for me and pushed his way in. He came to our room and asked if I am Ruth Wachner. He then told me that he had a message from my father. I got very excited and my hopes soared. He told me that he was together with my father and brother in Auschwitz. My father was actively involved to find an escape route for the young men in his barracks. He told me that my father kept their spirit alive with prayers and songs and hope. My father told all those people with him that if any of them survive they must look for me. He was sure that I would be alive. Then the young man proceeded to tell me that someone had found out about my father's activities and as an example for the other inmates my father was hanged on Yom Kipur 1943 in front of the assembled prisoners. My brother was then told to dig a grave, cut down my father and bury him. Then my brother, Benjamin Ben Jehoshua Hacohen, my Benno, was shot and thrown into the grave with our father, Jehoshua Ben Aaron Hacohen.

I went into shock and remember very little of what happened next. I started screaming and called him a liar. The landlady hearing my screams came in and scolded the young man and he left. Probably thinking that we were all mad. He never came back and I don't know his name and have no information about him. I wore myself out and fell into a deep sleep. When I awoke I told Tuska that I had had a terrible nightmare. Tuska just sat there and listened to me and kept shaking her head. It was not a nightmare she kept telling me. I was hysterical and she could not calm me down. She left me in the care of the landlady and ran to get David Tanzman. He got some sedatives from the medic and stayed with me for a long time. He came back every day and nursed me back to physical health but could do very little for my mental well-being. Did I ever fully recover from that shock? It took many years before I allowed myself to think about it or talk about it. One does not ever recover from this kind of shock.

During one of Dave's visits I told him that I will NEVER have children. I will not bring children into this world to expose them to so much pain. Dave listened patiently in his kind way and, when I calmed down, asked me, "And who will make this a better world?" He told me that there is a legend, which tells that there will always be 36 righteous people in the world whose purpose it is to rebuild and repair the world. It is called Tikun Olam. "Who knows why you survived," he said, "and what your offspring will do to better this world." Now, as I look at my children I am often reminded of his words. My children are indeed contributing to make life better for many families and thus in some small way are repairing the ills of the world. I take great comfort and pride in them.

I knew that Regina and Max Schneiderman with their children, Edith and Ben, had emigrated to America before the war. I did not know their address.

One of the Jewish officers, Jerry Bechhofer, put an ad in a German/English New York newspaper. It was called The *Aufbau* and was read by a large segment of New York Jews of German background. The housekeeper of the Schneiderman family was a lady (Mrs. Wasserhart) who read the paper and one day saw this ad. She arrived in the morning and told Regina that there is someone looking for a family, which they fit the description were it not for the fact that the last name is different. Their name in America was not Schneiderman (an assumed name in Germany) but Miller. I was soon contacted by them and arrangements were made to get me to America. Tuska was able to make contact with an uncle, the brother of her mother, and she too prepared to leave Germany. As long as we had someone to come to in the USA, our passage was paid for by the American Jewish Joint Distribution Committee.

We left Heidelberg at the end of May 1946 for a DP Camp in Bremen Hafen to await our passage to America. We were filled with hope, great expectations and impatient to leave Germany. The city of Bremen was totally destroyed and the rats were rampant. In the camp we met many people like us, awaiting passage. We had shelter and ample food and in the evening there were movies or other entertainment.

One evening I was leaving the movie theater to go back to our room. It was cool outside and I wanted to get a sweater. As I walked into the building a man came towards me. I looked at him and he looked at me from a distance of about 10 feet. We both stopped and stared at each other. Then he said "Malutka Rutka, to ty?" (Little Ruth, is that you?) I could not answer, my knees buckled and I went down on the floor. It was my first boyfriend, Zyga Steinhauer. He got down on the floor next to me, held me and we both cried. People came to us and at some point I was helped up and taken to my room. Zyga asked many questions and I told him as much as I knew. When I asked him about his family he told me that he was the only one who survived. He was stunned that I survived since I had been so close to death's door when he left. I was crying hysterically and soon a medic came and gave me a sedative that put me to sleep. The next morning Zyga came to me and told me that he was married and his wife is expecting a child. Her name was Ruth. My memory of Zyga was special. Our parents were very close friends and, as was customary in those days, children were often paired off. I had a crush on Zyga and he seemed equally fond of me. It seemed to our parents that this was a proper match. It was Zyga who introduced Benno and me to the Zionist organizations and we often talked about going to Palestine together, living on a kibbutz and building the country as predicted by Theordore Herzl. We were young chronologically, but our experiences with anti-Semitism added a measure of seriousness and maturity to our years. I walked around with a lump in my throat, pretended to be happy for him and his wife. Had I met him sooner, who knows what would have been? Or, had I not met him at all, I would not have resurrected him into my life.

Tuska and I got passage on the *Marine Perch* and arrived in the United States on June 19, 1946. We met Ernst Dannemann on board ship. He was Bureau Chief of AJDC in Frankfurt and was going home for his sister's wedding. He was very helpful to us and arranged for both of us to have some work at the Bursar's Office in exchange for which we got our own tiny little cabin (big improvement over steerage) and were invited to eat at the Captain's Table. Tuska and

Ruth wachner, Ernst Dannemann and Tuska Schmidt (aboard marine perch, destination USA, 1946)

Ernie fell in love and were married in August 1946, only two months after our arrival. At the pier we were met by our respective families: Tuska by her uncle and I by Tante Regina's husband Uncle Nathan Miller (formerly Max Schneiderman) and their son Ben.

On the way home in a taxi, Uncle told me not to talk about the war or the family. I was not to upset Tante and I was to forget all about what happened. Start a new life, forget everything, he told me. I was stunned. Both Tuska and I had such great expectations of loving, caring family. We were sure that they would want to hear all about our experiences, that they would cuddle us, take care of us and help us heal. I had memories of my own family's life, which was harmonious and loving. That is what I was looking forward to, that is what I craved and yearned for. It was not meant to be. When we arrived at their house I was greeted very warmly by Tante and Edith. We had a lovely lunch and after that Uncle asked me what I planned to do now that I am in America. I told him that I was told that school is free in America and I must go to school since my education ended prematurely and I need to learn a trade. He nodded his head approvingly and asked me, "And what will you live on while you go to school?" Suddenly the atmosphere became charged. It was a question I had never given any thought to. Tante was standing at the sink and when she heard him she yelled out "Max, what are you doing?" (Tante always called him Max, which was his name when she met him in Germany.) He turned to her, put his index finger to his mouth and said very sternly "schweig" (be silent). From that moment I realized my position.

Tante was sickly and although she was very loving to me I felt that I was an intruder. I slept on the living room couch with my suitcase in the corner. Many nights I cried myself to sleep.

Tuska's experiences were different yet similar. Her uncle had a big family and they were rather poor and lived in a very crowded little house. Tuska and I had planned to enroll in high school since we had no education. Luckily, we had taken English language and typing lessons before we left Heidelberg We needed to support ourselves and both got work in a publishing house at Stechert-Hafner, Inc., at 31 East 10th Street in Manhattan. We started to work the Monday after July 4. We found a room on 112th Street and Broadway in Manhattan, which we decided to rent together. When I announced my decision to move, Uncle had some very unpleasant words for me, which made Tante cry and leave the room. He told me that I was not welcome to come back to their house ever again. I was a bad influence on Edith he said. He also said that he knows the reason why I am moving. It is to continue whoring, which is probably how I survived the war. Someday I may be able to write more about this.

I left and shared the room with Tuska until she went back to Germany to join Ernie in the late fall of 1946. I could write a lot about my first winter in New York. I often said that it was the most difficult year of my life.

During the war, I went from one hour to the next, from one day to the next, never allowing myself to think. Now, I had to face the reality that I lost ALL my loved ones, that I was indeed all ALONE. I did not have enough money to pay for the room and food, and often walked home from work to save the nickel for a can of baked beans. Ernie's sister Hanna and her husband Fred Schweitzer were living nearby and many times when my loneliness (after Tuska's departure) got too oppressive, I would call Hanna and was always welcome to share a meal with them in their little room.

One evening I left work and started to walk back to my little room. I lived on 112th Street and Broadway and worked on 10th Street off University Place, a distance of over 100 blocks. It began to snow but I did not mind. A policeman on his beat stopped me and asked where I was going. When I told him where I lived he said that it is too far and I better get on the subway. We were expecting a blizzard and I had another 46 blocks to walk. I kept telling him that I was OK and liked walking in the snow. He walked a few blocks with me, stopped and took out a quarter from his pocket and gave it to me. I was stunned and asked for his address so I could send back the money to him. He then said, "Someday you will give it to someone who needs it, and you will pay it forward," and he left. I never forgot that angel in the midst of a blizzard. And yes, I did pay it forward many times thinking of him.

I continued to work. The following year, early 1947, requests for scientific magazines arrived from Poland, Germany and even Tel Aviv. I was able to handle those orders since I knew the languages. Almost overnight, my position changed. I was given a substantial wage increase and no longer had to worry about paying my rent or eating. In addition, Tante found a room for me in the Bronx, which was a lot cheaper then the one in Manhattan.

After a while, Tante insisted that I come up to the house and Uncle became more civil.

Irving and I met on August 1, 1947, and after a whirlwind courtship were married December 28, 1947. Regina Irene was born May 7, 1950. Susan Janet was born June 13, 1952, and Jay Benjamin was born January 24, 1956. My life was full, my cup was overflowing.

1983 Mothers Day:

No grave for my mother
No spot for me to place a stone
Plant a flower, pick a weed
Only the searing memory of her tender touch
Her last advice for me to heed.

No grave for my mother
No flower, no stones
Not even ashes of her bones.

No place for me to shed a tear
So distant the past, the pain so near.
No grave for MY mother!

I have completed the task I set out to do. I went over all my earlier notes as well as some of the later writings. I have tried to incorporate everything into this memoir. Some of the earlier dates may be inaccurate.

The pictures I was able to get from Uncle Solomon. The letter is the last one written by my mother to the woman (Pani Mania) who occupied the house with us during the German occupation in Brzostek. She mailed it to me after Uncle Siegmund retrieved the valuables and gave her my address in New York.

Did I ever resurrect God? The God of my childhood? Oh, He haunted me. On the first Yom Kipur in New York I was alone in my room. I decided to go to a synagogue, just to be with other people. I got dressed and walked until I found one. When I came to the entrance there was a guard in uniform at the door. He told me that I cannot go in unless I have a ticket. When I asked him where I can get a ticket he looked at me shook his head in wonderment and laughed. I saw him as "Satan" in uniform laughing at me. I left and walked towards the river and sat on a bench in Riverside Park. I sat and remembered holidays past and cried. I did not need a Minian to say Yiskor. I remembered everyone, sitting alone on that bench. The tears flowed freely while I watched the sun on the river and remembered. A policeman passed by, looked at me and walked on. After some minutes he came back and asked me if I was all right, if I needed help. I shook my head and he left me there. I remembered my family, my little town, my Brzostek, my Camelot. All doors were open for me there, everyone knew me and I was always welcome in every home. Now ALL doors were closed to me. I remembered the Polish teacher who would come for a cup of tea to visit with my mother. She would sit and say to her "Reginka, tell me about the big city, read to me." She was old and nearly blind. All the Lobel children were her pupils but she had a special affinity for my mother. My mother, the wonderful storyteller. I was overcome with aloneness. In this setting of normalcy for others, I was an outsider. I was an orphan, an orphan in history of 5000 years.

GOD, that childhood God would test me many times. On December 26 and 27, 1947, there was a big snowstorm. The biggest snowstorm New York ever had. I was getting married on December 28, and on that day the sun was shining brightly on the fresh snow. I was standing under the Chupah with my mate to be. When the Rabbi concluded the ancient priestly blessings I suddenly felt the shell, that shell that I had built up to keep God out, crack. Was God mocking me? Where is Pappa, my father who should be intoning these blessings? My father whose last words to me were the blessings and command to live and tell all. How could I "tell all" when no one wanted to listen?

The only one who wanted to hear and know all was my new husband. I felt the tears and pushed them back. How could I explain tears when everyone was shouting Mazal Tov? I was happy and grateful. So, did God have a hand in that? Was it God or was it ritual that I liked and wanted back? I was not quite ready to make peace with that elusive God.

Brzostek was still there but not for me. All the buildings are still there. Grandfather's house, Uncle Bergman's house, the post office, the church and adjacent school. Even the street leading to the big temple is still called "Ulica Zydowska" Jew Street. The temple is now a school. All is there but my people, ashes, they are all gone. Not even a grave where I could put a stone at a Yahrzeit.

When our son Jay became a Bar Mitzva I looked at that beautiful child named for my father and brother, Jehoshua Benjamin, and I finally made peace with God. A new God, a God I could forgive. I looked around, saw my husband, my two beautiful daughters and my son, and my friends around me. I turned to Tuska and told her that now, only now did I win the war. I won because I could forgive that elusive God.

I take a measure of pride that out of the chaos I was able to bring a sense of meaning to my life and create a future. Yes David, you were right. Our people have survived and kept history alive for over 5000 years. So have I! I have lost much, but I have never lost my personal integrity and morality. My early lessons have guided me well. I used to wonder if I would ever laugh again. Really laugh, like that time on the floor in our apartment in Berlin with Benno and Mutti. Well, you my children know that I did and still do with you.

Yes Papa, I have survived in the fullest meaning of the word and have told all who would listen and I have not forgotten!

With this, I a Bat Cohan, bless my children and grandchildren and bestow this legacy upon you.

For you my children who fill my life with joy;

For my husband for his love, encouragement and support;

For all those yet to come.

EPILOGUE

For many years Irving and I talked about going back to Poland one more time. Both of us had ambivalent feelings. Do we dare to open the door to the past? What will we find? Surely no one is there to welcome us. Then, we decided that we shall only go back if any of our children or grandchildren will show an interest in these places of our past.

On May 23, 2001, Irving, our daughter Regina, our two granddaughters Elana and Stephanie and I left New York for Poland. We arrived in Warsaw the next day, checked into our hotel and immediately proceeded to familiarize ourselves with the surroundings. Warsaw was rebuilt after the war and the city is beautiful. Large avenues lined with trees, shops busy with lookers and shoppers, and parks filled with elderly people and young children enjoying the balmy May afternoon. We passed a large building in the center of town, the cultural center erected during the Russian occupation. Right next to it a flea market busy with afternoon shoppers. The girls investigated for bargains while we rested in the park. We found a restaurant near the hotel, had an early dinner and called it a day.

The next day we went to find Anielevicz Place. As we were standing on the corner looking at our maps, a young man in his forties approached us and asked if we need help. He proceeded to lead us to our destination. He would not leave us alone to find our way and we became somewhat suspicious. What did he want? Why is he not at work? When we finally got to Anielevicz Square (the site of the former Warsaw Ghetto with a monument of Mordechai Anielevicz, the leader of the Warsaw Ghetto Uprising in April of

Ruth and Irving

1943) the man proceeded to say goodbye and gave us a message to take back to America. "Tell your friends and families that not all Poles are racist and anti-Semites, take this message home with you and do come back again."

We spent some time there, lit a candle, placed some stones on the monument and walked towards the Unschlagplatz. This is the place where people from the ghetto were brought after the uprising, to be transported to various concentration camps. The place is surrounded by walls and on one of the walls there is an inscription, a quote from the Book of Job, "Earth, do not cover my blood, and let no place exist to hear my cry." We sat quietly and I asked the girls, what do they hear? After a while they said that they heard silence and the noise of outside traffic. I told them then, that in the silence I hear cries, I hear the wails of mothers whose children were taken from them. I hear the commands of those with power to tear apart families and consider it a sport. In my mind's eye I see the square littered with baggage. Precious belongings, children's toys, a toy plane, a doll, a little shoe, all left there to be swept away.

After some more quiet moments we left in search of the only synagogue in Warsaw. It is active and has a kindergarten in full swing. It is non-denominational. The Este Lauder Foundation is supporting the few Jewish families who are actively involved in reviving a Jewish existence in a city which, before the war, had the largest number of Jews in all of Poland. It was Friday afternoon and the tables were set for an Oneg Shabbat. It would have been nice to stay but we had to catch a plane for Vilnius, Lithuania. We arrived in Vilnius late Friday evening.

When Irving was born and lived there the city was called Wilno and belonged to Poland. In 1939, when World War II started, the Russians occupied Wilno and shortly after handed the city over to Lithuania. Wilno was well known for its large and active Jewish community. It was the seat of Yiddish culture and birthplace of YIVO (Institute for Yiddish Cultural Research). It was the city known for the Wilno Goen, the Genius of Wilno, as well as the Shulhoyf, the synagogue courts, all symbols of religion and tradition. There were supposedly over 100 synagogues in Wilno. To Jews the city was knows as the "Jerushalaim de Lite", the Jerusalem of Lithuania. The late Rabbi Abraham Joshua Heschel wrote an essay on Jewish Wilno:

"With what shall I compare thee, Wilno, Holy Jewish community? Every Jew a page of the Talmud, a chapter of Psalms, a song of faith and sorrow, a silent cry, a humble chant.
And we did not then understand our treasure."

Oh yes, WE the survivors, WE know what was lost.

Saturday morning we went in search of, and under Irving's guidance found, the only surviving synagogue, the well-known "Chor Shul" (Choir Synagogue). Our friend, Sol Aaron, sang with the choir in this synagogue when he was a young boy. There were about 12 men at the Shabbat service. When the Gabbai (religious attendant) saw us enter he opened the women's section in an upstairs balcony. It was very dusty and neglected, no sign of attendance and we stayed but a few minutes. None of the men in the congregation were originally from Wilno. Most are Russian immigrants. It was quite depressing; especially for Irving, who remembered a very different atmosphere.

In the afternoon we went to Ponary. This is a forest about 20 kilometers outside of Wilno. In September 1943, all the Jews from the Wilno Ghetto were marched to that forest, machine-gunned down, thrown into a ravine and set on fire. Irving's father Schlomo, his sister Emma, her husband and their little boy Benjamin, and a number of cousins were among those killed there. It was cold and windy when we got there and our hearts were heavy and filled with sorrow. The girls picked up stones on the way and we all placed them on the monument erected there by the Israeli government. A sign that we were there and that they are not forgotten. Irving recited Kaddish, we held hands and cried.

The following day, Sunday, we walked all through the city. We went to the house where Irving was born. Not only was he born there but so was his father. We did not go inside, just walked around and listened to Irving's memories. We walked through the old city, former ghetto and Jewish section, visited Irving's elementary and high school and then walked up to the new city. Vilnius is a very beautiful city not yet spoiled by tourism. When we were there, there was a NATO meeting as well as an International Trade Show. It was impossible to get hotel reservations. We rented an apartment for two nights in the old city. A very old building but nicely renovated and we were quite comfortable. In the morning as we were leaving to tour the city our daughter found an old imprint on the right side of the old door. It was slanted and there was no doubt that it was the place of a former Mezuza. Whose house was it? Who had lived there? No answers to these questions.

Sunday evening we flew to Krakow, Poland. We arrived at midnight but were up early the next day.

We went by van to Auschwitz-Birkenau. What can I say about this place that has not been said already? I have seen pictures, read all about it, heard stories from survivors, but never could I have fully comprehended the enormity of that place and the enormity of the crimes committed there. We walked through the gates with the inscription "Arbeit Macht Frei" (work will set you free), and again I, I did not see the tourists around me. In my mind's eye I saw my father and brother and other family members walk this path to what became their last walk. What did they think? Did they chant psalms?

"The Lord is my shepherd; I shall not want;
He maketh me to lie down in green pastures;
He leadeth me beside still waters, He restoreth my soul;
He guideth me in straight paths for His name's sake;
Yea, though I walk through the valley of the shadow of death;
I will fear no evil for Thou art with...?"

Were they able to complete the sentence "For thou art with ME"? Or did they ask, "Where is MY God"?

Irving and I could not have made this trip alone. Having the children with us was an affirmation. WE ARE HERE, we are the spark, the amber which survived to rekindle the flame. We came to leave a stone from us for ALL our families who died there; to tell them that they are not forgotten. We shall not give Hitler posthumous victory. All around us we could see the partially destroyed remnants of man's inhumanity. We stood around the pits filled with ashes, ashes of our beloved families and here too we left stones on the monuments.

We held each other and cried bitterly. Until I saw that place it was only a figment of my imagination. Now reality took root. I shall never think of Auschwitz-Birkenau the same way.

The following day we walked through much of Krakow. We found the old Jewish section called Kazimierz. My mother's aunt (Regina Miller's mother) lived there. We used to visit her quite frequently. Yes, there too we found one remaining active Synagogue. It was closed by the time we got there. There was a sign in Yiddish, Polish and Hebrew telling people not to walk on the sidewalk. There were graves underneath the sidewalk which had been desecrated and paved over. Krakow was and still is a very beautiful city and it too was once a center of Jewish life and culture. It was painful to see that it is all gone. And yet, we are a stubborn people. We have survived and will continue in spite of all that happened and is still happening.

We went to a salt mine near Krakow called Wieliczka. I had been there with my class from school when I was 12 years old and remembered that trip. We went down to the lowest possible level of the mine. On each level there were niches with statues of the Trinity, all carved out of salt. Every level also showed carved dwarfs who, according to legend, helped the miners carry the salt to the top. At the very bottom, in the largest hall there was a carved statue of the present Pope, favored son of Poland. Our guide pointed to a Star of David on one of the walls. She told us that during the German occupation during WWII this hall was turned into a factory for airplane parts. Jews worked here in the bowels of the earth and never came up to see the light of day. When they could no longer work, they were brought up and sent to Birkenau for extermination. At the end of the war, before the last group was brought up they carved the Star of David on the wall in memory of all those who perished there.

The following day we hired a car with driver and drove to Brzostek. Brzostek was my Camelot. There are some scenes from my childhood that are etched into my memory. Every summer my family and I spent our vacations with my maternal grandparents in this little town. We would travel by train from Berlin (later from Katovice) to Tarnow and from there take a horse and buggy to Brzostek. As soon as we neared the little town my heart would race with anticipation. Would Grandmother be there waiting for us again as she always did? Would she call out excitedly to Grandfather in the store, "Bzalel, Rifka is du mit di Kinder," "Bzalel, Rifka is here with the children"? She never failed me. With wide-open arms she would come towards us, her cheeks flushed with excitement, hugging and kissing first us, my brother Benno and me, then Mother and then a friendly nod to Father. Grandfather would leave his customers and come out to kiss us children on the forehead and look at his favorite daughter and thank God for once more bringing us safely home. For this was always "home". Father and Benno would busy themselves with the luggage and I did not know where to run first. I had to inspect every corner of the house and garden in the back. I had to run all over the rynek (town square) to say hello to uncles, aunts and cousins. Before long, Grandfather would call Father and Benno, and together they went to synagogue for Mincha and Maariv, the afternoon prayers and also say a special prayer of thanks for our safe arrival. All along the road men would come out of their houses and join in. "Rifka is home" could be heard all along the road.

In 1942 I was forced to leave the little town and all whom I loved and who loved me, never to see them again, never to hear those words of welcome again. For sixty years I have thought about going back once more. All those years I harbored a vision in my mind's eye. Grandfather Bzalel in his long Shabbos coat with the gartel (braided silk belt) around his waist and schtrahmel (hat with fur trim) on his head. He is holding Grandmother Rudeh's hand. She is wearing her best dress and sheytel (wig) with the paisley shawl with long fringes around her shoulders. They seem to be floating above the houses looking down, looking for their children, looking for their Rifka with her children and waiting, waiting, waiting.

I cannot bring back your Rifka, I tell them in my many sleepless nights. But wait, I tell them, I will bring you MY Rifka, your great granddaughter, and I will bring great great grandchildren. You were with me, I tell them, in Jerusalem for the Bar Mitzvahs of two of your great great grandsons. I felt you near me, you were with me in the ancient city, you never left me.

And now, in the year 5761, corresponding to the year 2001, now I have brought you MY Rifka, named for your beloved daughter and my two granddaughters Stephanie (Sara) and Elana. Now we are here, now the cycle is complete, now you can rest in peace, I tell them for the last time.

After sixty years I returned to Poland, the land that did not want me, for a brief visit. I came back with deep scars but also with new life. Sometimes the past returns as present. I needed to come back. I needed to place stones on places of memory erected for my people. Here, in Brzostek, there are no personal graves, there are no tomb stones, they were used as foundations for new houses. And there are no monuments.

Somewhere, deep inside of me, I feel that they know, that ALL my people know. THEY know that some one cared enough to come at least once to say a silent Kaddish.

ADDENDUM

December 2011.

I have given a lot of thought to the chapter, which I am about to write. It has a place in the pages of my history. Ten years ago these accounts might have hurt somebody. Now, no one is alive to be hurt and I believe there is a lesson to be learned.

If you go back to page 93 you will note that I said, "Someday I may be able to write more about this." I think, now in the winter of my life, is the time.

Uncle Solomon, Uncle Joseph, and my father were very close. Tante had Uncle Solomon's address and in 1946 I established contact with him in what was then Palestine. He and his family lived in Tel Aviv. He suggested that I go to America since there was no legal way he could get me to Tel Aviv at that time. It would be easier for me in America.

In 1966 Uncle Solomon went to Switzerland and then came to America. He stayed with us and was rather surprised how modestly we lived. Irving worked two jobs and I worked part time. One day he asked me to drive him to see the Millers. I made the arrangements for a visit. When we got to Great Neck where they lived, Uncle Solomon told us to stay downstairs since he had some private business to discuss. We were rather surprised but did as he asked. After about half an hour we decided to go up and see what was going on. It was rather strange. When we got off the elevator we heard shouting from

Nathan and Regina Miller (1965)

the apartment and went back to the car. After some 15 minutes Uncle Solomon came down and we went home. He was visibly upset but did not wish to discuss his visit.

In 1967 Uncle (Miller) had his first stroke followed by two more strokes in 1969.

Tante went into a deep depression and no matter what I did I could not help her. She refused to get help and scolded me for being too much involved. It is not you who should be with me but my children she said repeatedly. Unfortunately it was a time when Edith and Ben were having their own problems and since they lived in Princeton and Boston visits were very infrequent.

On the second day of Rosh Hashana in the year 1969 Tante (Regina Miller) committed suicide. She left a note saying, "I am taking care of myself." I had to identify her, and Irving and I made funeral arrangements and arranged for Uncle Nathan to be transferred to a local nursing home, which would make it easier for us to look after him.

Ben asked me to come to the bank with him. He opened the safety deposit box and among some very nice jewelry there was a bank book. It was in Tante's name in trust for me. It had very small deposits ($3.– to $5.–, never more than $10.– at a time) beginning in 1946. The total in 1969 came to almost $18,000.00 Ben was shocked. For you? What about me and my children? How about Edith? Why you? He called his mother crazy and told me that he would challenge this. I did not have an answer for him. Since there was no will it took many years before I got the money minus all the legal fees.

In December 1969 Irving and I went to Israel for a visit. Uncle Solomon got sick. The day before we were to leave for home we went to see him. He was bedridden and asked me to come to the bedroom alone. He had some important information for me. I asked to have Irving with me and he agreed. He then told us that in 1938 my father deposited $20,000.00 via Switzerland into a bank account established by Nathan Miller. It was to be a safety net for us if and when any of us came to America. Uncle Solomon told us that when he questioned Uncle (Miller) about it in 1966 his answer was that he needed the money and used it to support his family and to bring me to America.

The truth is that the affidavit that he sent me, which promised that I would never be a ward of the government, had cost him no more than the fee of a notary public. I was a refugee and my passage from Germany to America was paid for fully by the American Joint Distribution Committee for whom I had worked in Heidelberg for 10 months.

I went into shock and did not stop crying for the entire trip home. How was I going to face the man who cheated me out of an education? The man who maligned me in front of his family? The man who contributed to my hardship that first year in America? How was I going to take care of him knowing what I knew now?

Shortly before landing I turned to Irving and told him that we shall continue to take care of him because it is the right thing to do. Irving said that he knew I would do that but, it had to be my decision. I said that Uncle (Miller) was punished more severely than anything we could do. His wife committed suicide rather than take care of him and his children had no interest and never came to see him. They knew that I was there.

You my children know that we took care of him. He was with us for holidays. Irving would wheel him over for family cookouts and we even made him a birthday party. We made arrangements for our doctor to look in on him and made sure that he was well cared for. There were days he would call me complaining about some discomfort or pain and I would always go to see him. Most of the time these were false alarms; he just wanted my attention.

Nathan Miller died in February 1971. We made all the arrangements and Ben came for the funeral but did not stay for Shiva. Edith did not come.

I said that there was a lesson to be learned here. Earlier in my memoirs I wrote about the day when Tuska, Rose and I refused to take anything from the German woman. We would not do what was done to us. And so, here too, my early lessons of morality and ethics guided me on a righteous path. "That which is hateful to you, do not do onto others."

This might well be my last entry into this book. I have one more task to do. And that is to put a plaque on a tombstone with the names of my ancestors in the cemetery in the town of Brzostek. The stone will include the names of Tantes' parents. I pray that I shall be able to do what I set out to do. If not, it is a task I leave to you my children.

IT IS DONE.

On June 17, 2012, corresponding to the Hebrew year 5772 we attached a plaque to a tombstone in the Jewish cemetery in Brzostek. It is dedicated by me to the memory of the Lobel, Schlanger and Licht families. I always felt that since I am the only witness who survived, I have an obligation to do something special. And now I did it.

This would not have been possible but for the efforts by the Jewish Heritage Project to restore the Jewish cemetery in the town of Brzostek, The ceremony was attended by my own family and extended families who came from Israel, South Africa, France, Belgium, Australia and the United States. We said El Mole Rachamim and Kadish led by the Polish Chief Rabbi Michael Schudrich.

In attendance was the Deacon of the Parish of Brzostek, Fr. Dr. Jan Cebulak as well as Mayor Leszek Bieniek of Brzostek and the Town secretary Mrs. Lucyna Pruchnik.

Reclaimed Jewish cemetery in the town of Brzostek (June 2012)

That same day we also attended a memorial service at the mass grave in the Podzamce forest where about 260+ Jews were murdered in 1942. How many of them were my family? In attendance were close to 50 descendants from nine countries. We wept openly as some of the names of the families that were murdered there were intoned, one by one, in the traditional Jewish Memorial Service. At the end, the sound of the Shofar was heard throughout the forest. An affirmation that our loved ones are not forgotten, that we are here.

So, this is the end of MY story. I am forever grateful that I was able to accomplish, with the support and help of my family, what I set out to do. There is a rumor that there will be a film about Brzostek. I think the town was a prototype of Jews and Christians living in relative harmony for nearly 900 years. Whatever happens in the future concerning this little town of Brzostek (my own Camelot) will tell its own story.

AFTERWORD

I remember one Rosh Hashonah, sitting alongside my parents, in our synagogue, Temple Beth El of Rockaway Park, when my mother turned towards me, looked at her three adult children, her eight grandchildren, and with a sense of pride and accomplishment whispered in my ear: "Who has had a better life than me... Am I not the luckiest woman in the world?" This stunned me at first, knowing what she had endured, how she suffered and what was stolen from her. But I quickly realized, that this statement summarizes my mother's life, her strength, her optimism, her spirituality and why so many think of her as an angel on earth.

My mother's life in America has been and continues to be wonderful and productive. She married my father, Irving, on December 28, 1947 and 63 years later, to the day, buried him alongside my brother's son, Jonathan, who died when he was two and half. During the week of Shiva my mother told us that my father was the love of her life. It was only after he died that she began to feel her age. My father was a humble, quiet man, who made my mother, his children and grandchildren always feel safe. My father was the first person who listened to my mother, who held her while she remembered the unbearable, who awakened her from her frequent nightmares and who helped her heal. He was tender towards her, and in their final years together, every night before they went to sleep he would take her hand and kiss it.

Together my parents lived the American dream. They arrived with no money or worldly possessions and through hard work, a powerful commitment to one another and their family, began the rebirth process.

My parents lived a life of Tikun Olam. They raised three productive, accomplished children, who in turn brought them nine grandchildren. My mother would often tell my brother, sister and me, that the Nazis took everything that her family owned, but they could never rob her of her education. Her knowledge of Torah continues to amaze.

In 1959 we moved from a housing project in the Bronx to the home in Belle Harbor, Queens, where my mother continues to live. She still enjoys her daily walks along the beach, which she calls her therapy. My parents were known and loved in this community and their synagogue.

My mother received a high school equivalency diploma in the early 1950s and went to college in the 1970s. She became a dental hygienist and practiced for over 30 years alongside her dear friend Danny Staub. Danny and his wife Mimi became close friends, along with Frieda and Sol Aaron, Arlene and Ira Levy, Alex and Dottie Miller, Sherwin and Lillian Arnold, and scores of others. People were drawn to my parents, particularly my mother, who, among her many accomplishments, is a wonderful cook and baker. Our home was always the meeting place, where friends and family would gather for delicious meals and evenings of songs and merriment. My sister and I would play the piano and we would often have sing-alongs. Every Friday night was a holiday. My mother loves the Opera and classical music, and our house was filled with music. To this day classical music plays throughout the day and every Saturday afternoon she listens to live broadcasts from the Metropolitan Opera or other opera houses.

I remember my mother's commitment to social issues, she championed school integration, and was part of the Peace Movement of the 1960's. My parents instilled in their children and grandchildren a love of Israel. When they were in their sixties they decided to volunteer on Kibbutz Parod, and did so for eight summers. They worked with me and my first husband, Gil, in our special education camp and are still remembered by many of the campers. Together

Pagirsky-Skyer-Foley family (September 2011)

Jay, Jeremy, Matt and Jamie Pagirsky (June 2010)

they travelled the world and found beauty and joy in all that they saw and did.

By the time my mother was in her sixties she started lecturing school children on the Holocaust. My father would drive her wherever she was invited. She particularly liked speaking to non-Jewish audiences. She would ask students to write to her after she spoke and until their tragic loss in Hurricane Sandy in 2012, she had a collection of thousands of letters in her basement, attesting the impact that she had on her audiences.

I could go on and on providing examples of my mother's positive commitment to life and to people. I want the readers of this book to understand the words my mother often uses. She says: "The Holocaust defined me, but it did not destroy me." In spite of all she suffered, my mother always saw and continues to see the goodness in people, the goodness of God and the beauty in our world.

- *Regina Skyer*

January 2013

17685568R00064

Made in the USA
Middletown, DE
04 February 2015